THE MACHINE IN THE GHOST

THE MACHINE IN THE GHOST

DIGITALITY AND ITS CONSEQUENCES

ROBIN BOAST

reaktion books ltd

For Rosita and Filippo,
who put up with everything

Published by
REAKTION BOOKS LTD
Unit 32, Waterside
44–48 Wharf Road
London N1 7UX, UK
www.reaktionbooks.co.uk

First published 2017
Copyright © Robin Boast 2017

Printed and bound in Great Britain by Bell & Bain, Glasgow

A catalogue record for this book is available from the British Library

ISBN 978 1 78023 739 8

CONTENTS

INTRODUCTION

T his is a book about the *digital*, or, rather, about how digitality emerged from a complex set of technologies, circumstances, social and economic needs and desires over the past 150 years. The digital that I explore in this book is not about fingers; neither is it about numbers, nor even necessarily about computers or computation. It is about the encoding that underlies all of the technologies that today we refer to as 'digital'. This is not *the* history of digitality, but *a* history: my wandering through a tangled social and technological land-scape that has emerged, in a complex way, since the mid-nineteenth century, and its consequences for what we do, and can do, with digital technologies.

I have spent my life in this increasingly digital world, and have spent all of my professional life working with what we now call digital tech-nologies. Many of you who find yourselves reading this book will have spent your entire life surrounded by the digital. You are of the digital generation, whose lives have been completely engaged with digital devices, digital services and digital objects. By contrast, I did not personally encounter the digital until I was in my early teens. That was over forty years ago, and, aside from a few of my friends in high school, none of the rest of my fellow students had at that time had any direct encounter with digitality. So the small group of five of us, and one teacher, who would sit around our terminal, with its modem link to the University of Colorado mainframe, were part of a very small collective who had actually worked with the digital.

Today, of course, it would be hard to find anyone who has not had some direct engagement with the digital. There are few people in the world who do not have some sort of digital identity, for we don't need to own any devices for us to exist digitally. Even if we are not online, and do not have our own digital space, we all have multiple digital identities that have been recorded by official agencies in multiple databases, logs and official digital documents. It would be hard, if not impossible, to find anyone who was not part of the vast digital archive in some form.

Those of us who use digital devices regularly are all digitally competent if not actually fluent. However, few would actually be able to come up with more than a cryptic definition of 'digital'. We are told that digital technologies are about computing or computation, yet few of us use these ubiquitous technologies to compute. Of course, we do occasionally use the calculator app that hides inside our Utilities folder. We may even use a spreadsheet from time to time, or even regularly in our work, but even then the vast majority of work done on spreadsheets involves tables – tabulation – not calculation or computation. Do any more than a few of us routinely use these technologies to compute? No. If what we mean by *computing* is not simply using these essentially algorithmic devices, which process digital codes via logic circuits, to compute or calculate, but using them for the vast diversity of media and communication work that we do with these devices, then an interesting thing about digital computing is how little computing – computation, reckoning, calculation – actually goes on. What is even more interesting, in my mind, is how little computing, in this sense, ever went on with these digital technologies. In fact, digital technologies, and digital media, have had very little to do with computation, ever.

So, this begs the question, what is the digital? What is digitality? We all have a basic idea that the digital, digitality, has something to do with computers, which have something to do with binary numbers, 1s and 0s. However, beyond this folkloric understanding, the vast majority of people have little idea what is going on inside their multitude of digital devices, digital services and digital documents. This is not their fault, as one of the defining qualities of contemporary digital technologies is that there is an enormous remove between what we do when we use these media devices and how they work – between superstructure and infrastructure. This separation was, in fact, an achievement. It was not always so, which is one of the points that I wish to discuss in this book. Our remove from the insides of digitality, from the infrastructure, was something designed and built, not a natural feature of digitality or digital technologies. In fact, early on, this remove was seen by many as downright undesirable.

Though one of the points of this book is that computing, in its generic sense, has very little to do with computation, what I primarily seek to do here is to provide an understanding of what digitality is – or, more accurately, what it was and what it has become. But don't we know what the digital is? We are told, from innumerable sources, authoritative and marginal, that digitality is 1s and 0s, binary numbers, or more broadly the storage of information as 1s and 0s. We are told that digital is a term for a technology, or set of technologies, that creates, stores, processes and transmits data in electronic 1s and 0s. The problem with this conventional definition is that it conceals more than it reveals.

First of all, when we store or process digital data we are not storing or processing 1s and 0s. We are storing and processing ons and offs, the mere presence or absence of something: in the case of computers, the presence or absence of an electronic charge. These ons and offs, by themselves, carry no information beyond this. They are the simplest forms of information – which is important nonetheless. Second, the ons and offs, which are generated, stored, transmitted and processed as signals, are not really 1s and 0s. Not to go into too much detail at the beginning, they are analogue potentials that the hardware interprets, electronically, as ons and offs. This is important, as the simplistic notion of the digital conceals the messy and complex reality that exists inside our digital devices. Finally, it also conceals the fact that even after the messy and complex reality of electrical potentials is translated by our devices into ons and offs, they still are not 1s and 0s. These ons and offs, the presences and absences, by themselves, do nothing.

However, what makes the digital, as we use it today, *digital* is that the combination of ons and offs, in very specific albeit complex ways, encodes information. Over the past 150 years these codes have encoded all types of information, including all of our media. Translating or encoding something, a mediation, into a code of ons and offs – this is digital, and this is the foundation of all digital technology. This is what it has become, and to a large degree what it always was – a media technology.

By following a series of historical tracks that start some way in the past and finish, often through complex and convoluted routes, in the present, I pick my way through this historical landscape. This is an account of what digitality was and what it became. In this way, I wind up trying to define what digitality is through its qualities that it shares with all media, but also by defining the qualities that are unique to digitality. What is it that makes the digital *digital*?

Why a history of digitality?

Why should we be interested at all in the history of the digital, any history? Isn't it enough to know that the digital has succeeded, that digitality and computation are natural products of progress and technological development? Often the marketing of digital technologies, media and services encourages us to believe this. Often our governments and policy-makers would also like us to believe it. We are told that we live in a digital age, work in a digital economy, are entertained exclusively, these days, by digital media and that our lives and our security can be indefinitely improved by the digital. Perhaps the corporations, governmental organizations and policy-makers actually do believe this. However, there is nothing natural or inevitable about the digital; nor was there anything inevitable about its development. The world we live in today, digital and non-digital, could have been otherwise. Often, but for some rather coincidental, perhaps fortuitous, events and circumstances, it could have been radically different. Mostly, though, it is important to tell these stories because, in their absence, many tall tales, based mainly on conjecture or conviction, get told, retold and taken for truth.

For example, digitality is much older than you may suspect. Going back to its origins, as digital encoding, we find the first digital media devices being developed in the 1870s. This is not a matter, as so often happens in conjectural histories of technologies, of shining the light of the present back in time and selecting anything that reflects back as an ancestor, regardless of whether it is historically, technologically or even conceptually linked in any way. The digital technologies of today have a clear genealogy going back to telecommunications technologies of the later nineteenth century.

However, the history I am telling here should not be read as the history. There are many different strands to the history of what today we call digital media, digital technologies and digitality. Some of these influence each other all the way through, while others have their day and disappear. Yet others quietly trundle along, largely unnoticed, until they find that they are appropriated to make a surprising, and perhaps monumental, contribution to the unfolding biography. Innovations, discoveries and new insights leap up, often from the most unlikely places, to transform and integrate disparate technologies and media into a new federation, opening up whole new possibilities and directions. However, to do so, they have to mobilize, in some way, vast communities of engineers, financiers, officials and users, as well as requiring the right materials and technologies to be available then, not later.

I have chosen some of these strands, and have developed them into a more or less understandable tangle, giving some strands precedence and others less than their due, while some I have left out altogether. All that has happened from the first digital encoding telegraphs to today's complex and manifold digital media, technologies, networks and systems, as well as their politics and social manifestations, could fill a library, and in its entirety would not make for very interesting reading. This is an account of the history of digitality, my account – an account that I hope makes sense, is interesting and is faithful to the evidence. You can read it without needing to have an academic or a technical background. Anyone should be able to pick up this book and learn something about digitality, or, at least, about its history.

But why should we go so far back in history, back into the nineteenth century? Why not, as most histories of digitality do, look for its incorporation into electronic computers? Isn't that where it all *really* begins? But, then, why did computers become digital, and, more importantly, why did they become media machines? This too was not inevitable. If we wish to seek the qualities of the digital, and not just trace events as self-evident progress, it is best to start from its origins – not to define its origins for the sake of it, but to identify where and how these early technologies arose, for what purposes and ends, to perform what work and services. The foundations, formation and development of the digital, of digitality, give us key insights into what it was for, what its purposes and potentials were and why it was later appropriated in the ways that it was. If we seek the biographies of the medium, its qualities will be revealed.

A major problem is that histories of the digital are mired in a pretence that computing and computation provide the consequential qualities of digitality. However, if we look at the digital itself as an encoding medium, we find something very interesting. Digital code, the ons and offs that are stored on your hard drive, USB pen or, if you still have some, your DVDs, are unreadable to humans in their digital state. That seems obvious enough. The encoding of the information and the processing instructions are not meant to be read by any person. They are meant to be read by a mechanism that processes them and presents us with something that we can read, view or interact with that is meaningful to us as human beings. This is the genius of the digital that today is processed by means of electronic computers.

However, this is not the complete story. In fact, there is one form of digital encoding, the oldest, that we could in principle read directly. It wouldn't be easy and it would take a great deal of practice, but a large group of people did it before as part of their job, so we could do it again. This form is character encoding – the digital encoding of numbers and letters. Digital encoding of alphanumeric characters has been around for over 140 years. Some say it is older, if you accept Francis Bacon's cipher of 1605, which used As and Bs, as digital, or even Carl Friedrich Gauss and Wilhelm Weber's electromechanical system erected in Göttingen in 1833. I don't, so I would place the first real digital encoding with the invention of a Frenchman in the early 1870s.

Why is it, then, that we can read, or possibly read, digital alphanumeric codes and not other digitally encoded information? Why is it that we cannot look at the digital of a digital image and recognize what the image is? How is it that digital encoding does not represent that which it refers to? Why does the digital code of a digital image bear no direct resemblances to, representations of, the image we see? The answers lie both with the origins of the digital itself and what digital encoding was originally devised to do, as well as how it came to be used when integrated with electronic computers.

Machine in the ghost

In his book *Being Digital* (1995), Nicholas Negroponte, founder and long-time director of the MIT Media Laboratory, made a key distinction between atoms, the world of things, and bits, the world of the digital.

> The methodical movement of . . . most information in the form of books, magazines, newspapers, and videocassettes, is about to become the instanteous [sic] and inexpensive transfer of electronic data that move at the speed of light . . . the change from atoms to bits is irrevocable and unstoppable.[1]

This distinction, made early in the Web era, and somewhat acquisitive, between the world of physical things and the world of virtual, ephemeral, digital things, was not new and continues to pervade our understanding of new media, the Internet, e-commerce and social computing, as well as the *insides* of digital technology generally. When we think of digital things – our emails, images, videos, documents or

Facebook pages – we are asked to think of things that we interact with, but which are somehow not physical. They are electronic, ephemeral, ghostly. They arise from a technology that most of us do not really understand, and we believe has arisen from an elite world of mathematics and engineering – despite the fact that we are all experts at using it. The generic term for the machinery that this virtual ghost resides in is 'computing', or often 'computation'. Whatever it is that goes on inside our devices, we are told, has something (or other) to do with this ghostly process of computation, the processing of numbers by mathematics held in virtual – electronic – suspension. In other words, the digital is indelibly associated with a ghostly world, a world of virtuality. But is this all really so? Are there really ghosts in our machines?

The title of this book is *The Machine in the Ghost*. This alludes to a phrase that the exceptional twentieth-century philosopher Gilbert Ryle coined in his 1949 book *The Concept of Mind*.[2] His book was about René Descartes, the seventeenth-century philosopher, and his distinction between the mind and the body. Remember 'I think, therefore I am'? Put simply – far too simply – Descartes made a distinction between the physical world, which he characterized as a machine, and the mind, which he saw as ephemeral, immaterial, ideal – as the soul. Ryle characterized Descartes' separation of the mind (the ghost) from the body (the machine) as a 'category mistake', a philosophical error where the nature of the things being compared is misrepresented. According to Ryle, Descartes' characterization of the mind as a ghostly category, a soul, inside the machine of the body, 'the ghost in the machine' as Ryle characterized it, was confused about both what the mind is and what the body is.

As with Descartes' idealistic separation of the mind from the body, so we find a separation of virtual digitality from the mechanistic computing technology. As Descartes put a ghost in the machine, so have the prevailing accounts of digitality put a digital (virtual) ghost into the electronic computing machine. However, the assumption that the digital is virtual, by virtue of its encoding, makes the same category mistake as Descartes. In this book, I try to show that the virtual ghost of digitality is very real, very physical, and very active in the constitution of our contemporary digital world. It is not just that the digital is real, physical and tangible, but that hiding it from view is something fairly new, and it took, and still takes, a great deal of effort. It is not that digitality is essentially some unseen ghostly presence in our digital technologies, but that it is a mode of encoding media, and processing it, whose infrastructure, at one time visible, is now hidden. It is hidden by choice, not necessity, but it potentially remains as accessible to all of us as it once was.

It was the philosopher Gilbert Ryle's goal to expose Descartes' ghost in the machine as a confusion of what thinking is by focusing on the ghost, the ideas, to demonstrate that there is no ghostly mind. I wish to focus on the machine, on the many machines, devices and systems that have fortuitously, sometimes enigmatically, come together to form our contemporary digital world, to demonstrate that they too are but mere mechanisms, strategies and actions, in the world.

What I seek to do in this book, by virtue of following a number of complexly connected historical tracks of the digital, is to show that there is no ghost in our machine. Our digital devices, our multitude of digital machines, contain no ghostly presence. This false separation fundamentally misrepresents what the digital is, how it has developed and, therefore, how we all use it. More importantly, it continues to misrepresent the digital in a way that limits what we can do with it, and who can do what. The view of digitality as virtual doesn't just hide the digital infrastructure, it blocks most of us from actually working with it to its full potential.

Perhaps this is the goal of hiding digitality from its vast number of users. Perhaps the purpose is to keep most of us away from the digital, disempowered in our abilities to mould and forge our digitalities for our own ends. I am not a big fan of conspiracy theories. At my age, I have learned that most of what we may have thought were conspiracies turn out to be the consequences of ineptitude. I do not doubt that the vast majority of the proponents of the virtual are sincere. My goal here is not to chastise them, but to demonstrate that they are mistaken. That their virtual ghost is but a machine. The goal of this book is to show that the digital is corporeal; to expose the machine in the ghost.

1
DIGITAL CODES, TICKER TAPE, PUNCHED CARDS AND TELEPRINTING: ON THE ORIGIN OF DIGITALITY

There is not really a lot written about digitality or even the digital. To be sure, there is an abundance of texts, sites, blogs, dictionary entries, articles and books on *digital data*, *digital computing*, *digital media* or just about anything else that could use digital as an adjective. But just what is digitality if we think of it as a noun? What is *digital*? Even Wikipedia doesn't help much. When I typed in 'digital' no Wikipedia page resulted. I got a range of possibilities, though: digital data, digital computer, digital electronics, digital media and digital signal. I even found that *digital* could refer to *Digital: A Love Story*, a 2010 indie video game by Christine Love.[1] However, no helpful page of definitions, histories and other associations of the thing we call *digital*.

When you do start to piece together the bits that talk about digitality or the digital, you find that they tend to refer to a history, a genealogy, firmly attached to the beginning of electronic computing. If we go the formal definitional route, the *Oxford English Dictionary*, it seems that *digitality* has not yet arrived, officially, in the English language. We do find *digital*, however, with its uses as nouns and as adjectives. But even here in the definitive dictionary of the English language, we find *digital* qualifying forms of technology, most of which relates to computation or computers. There is reference to fingers and numerals below 10, even keyboards, but in the bastion of authoritative definitions, *digitality* seems to be firmly dependent on computation.

Histories of computing, which should shed light on digitality, are not much better. They refer loosely to the origins of the digital in Morse's code, in the Jacquard loom and its foreshadowing of the punched card revolution of the twentieth century. Basically, anything that made a beep or punched a hole, and could carry information as a result, seemed to be a direct and self-evident forebear of the digital. But even if we accept that these beeping and hole-punching technologies of the nineteenth century inevitably led to digitality as we understand it today, which we are not going to do here except for the sake of argument, then what did all this beeping and hole-punching have to do with computation?

Of course this somewhat flippant aside is to draw our attention to what I argue are the demonstrable qualities of the digital. Here we will look at the nineteenth-century beeping and hole-punching technologies, but from a different perspective: that of what they did to develop the idea that messages, the printed word in particular, could be *encoded* and transmitted electrically over vast distances very rapidly; that it was both possible, and a good idea, to develop an encoding medium that allowed people to communicate written messages over wires.

Please note that in this chapter we will not discuss any of the computational technologies as forerunners, or forefathers, of the digital. In the nineteenth century there was a great deal of interest in computers, computation and algorithmic processes, but, as we will find out, these did not directly influence the digital – at least not until the mid-twentieth century. The nineteenth-century technologies we are going to explore in this chapter only dealt with these matters tangentially. It is the world of telegraphs and telecommunications – the premier technological and economic revolutions of the nineteenth century – that we will discuss.

Morse wasn't digital

It was the new year 1825 when Samuel Morse, a portrait painter from Philadelphia in the relatively new United States, wrote to his wife, Lucretia, 'I have just learned in confidence [that I have been given the commission], from one of the members of the committee of the corporation appointed to procure a full-length portrait of Lafayette.'[2] The Lafayette referred to was none other than Marie-Joseph-Paul-Yves-Roch-Gilbert du Motier de Lafayette, the Marquis de Lafayette, who was a general in the American Revolution and close friend of George Washington. Known simply as Lafayette in the USA, he was a real celebrity, and gaining the commission to paint his portrait was a considerable achievement for Morse.

Morse travelled to Washington, DC, where Lafayette was staying at the time, on 4–6 February that year, meeting with him on the 9th to begin the portrait. By all accounts, the meeting went well, and Morse and Lafayette would strike up a friendship that would last until Lafayette's death in 1832. However, the day after Morse arrived in Washington, his father sent him an urgent letter imparting the tragic news of his wife's sudden death. He did not receive the letter until Friday 11 February, whereupon he immediately left for the long trip back to Philadelphia.[3]

Today, we only have the faintest understanding of what it must have been like to communicate with our families while travelling in the 1820s. We have a vague understanding that it took a long time to get somewhere, and that communications, by letter or courier only, also took a long time. We may be surprised, when we recount Morse's tragedy, that he and his family were corresponding with each other on almost a daily basis, albeit with the letters taking three or more days to travel the 225 km between Washington and Philadelphia. We can only imagine what it must have been like for Samuel Morse to make the three-day journey back to Philadelphia to his three children, the youngest only a few weeks old, to find his wife had already been buried two days previously.

There are two ways of thinking about this story. First, it is a common tale of a time when life expectancy, especially for childbearing women, was not long and communication over distance was lengthy. Even by the early 1800s, correspondence from Asia to North America, or Europe, would take a minimum of two months. That would be a third of a year for a letter to be sent from, say, Australia to England and a reply to return. That is, of course, if you were one of the very few people who could even afford to send a letter at all. The second way of thinking about this particular story is from Morse's own point of view, for it was Samuel Finley Breese Morse (1791–1872) who was one of the key players who would go on, over the next fifteen years, to utterly transform this situation and initiate the establishment of modern telecommunications. For Samuel Morse, our portrait painter from Philadelphia, is the Samuel Morse of Morse code fame and the single wire telegraph.

Legend has it that it was the death of Morse's dear wife that motivated him to explore the possibility of electrical communication. There is, however, no real evidence for this, and Morse never alluded to this event as related in any way to his later work on electromagnetism and the telegraph. A more likely impetus was his meeting with Charles Thomas Jackson while sailing back from a European trip in 1832. Jackson was a geologist who had an expert knowledge of electromagnetism and was the inventor of Jackson's electromagnet. It seems that their long conversations aboard ship sparked the keen interest of Morse, who began experimenting with electromagnets upon his return to New York. Also important was the help of Morse's colleague Professor Leonard Gale, a professor of chemistry at New York University, who put Morse in touch with developments in telegraphy and relays in Europe. Despite having very little in the way of scientific or technical competencies, Morse managed, by 1837, to create a working telegraph that could transmit a message over 16 km.

This achievement was not his alone; such achievements never are of one person. Morse was a driving force and seemed to have a knack for building collaborations with really talented people. The development of the Morse key, for example, went through several working versions, each one improved by people Morse was working with, or who were working for him. Critical improvements were made by his hired assistant, Alfred Vail. Batteries and key relay technology were provided by the collaboration with Professor Gale. When Morse actually won a grant from the U.S. Congress to run a test telegraph from

Baltimore to Washington, DC, the telegraph which is now portrayed as the '1st Telegraph', he employed a farmer from upper New York State to lay the cable in the ground using a plough. The project faced disaster when Morse realized that the cable in the ground would not work over more than 10–12 km. The day after the test, which demonstrated that Morse would soon be bankrupt, the farmer, a Mr Ezra Cornell, intentionally drove his plough into a rock, a pretence that gave precious time to devise a solution. Cornell's solution was to string the wire between posts on glass insulators above ground. The wire would soon transmit what was the first electric coded message, 'What hath God wrought!', sent by Morse from the Library of Congress to Alfred Vail in Baltimore on 24 May 1844. Ezra Cornell would go on to dominate the telegraph industry, ultimately forming, with partners, the Western Union company and donating a large portion of his fortune to found a university in his home town of Ithaca, New York.

Of course, it wasn't really the telegraph device that made Morse's name, though the basic design of the Morse key remains in use even today. The key invention of Morse's telegraph was a code, Morse's code. Morse's first code, one that he devised soon after his opportune return from Europe to New York, was a code to transmit numbers. The idea, which was not uncommon at the time, was to create a dictionary of common words and phrases, each indexed with a number. As the telegraph would be expensive and transmissions not very fast, the idea was to transmit the numeric codes, which would be looked up in a dictionary at the receiving end and then written down. It was Morse's assistant, Alfred Vail, who saw both the potential of an alphanumeric code, a code of both letters and numbers, and actually devised what we know today as Morse's code – the varying sequences of dots and dashes.

The key advantage of Morse's telegraph, unlike competing telegraphs in Europe, such as the Cooke and Wheatstone system which had been installed in London just a few years before, was that it offered a relatively rapid and easily learned code of letters and numbers for any form of message to be sent between operators electrically over a wire. Another advantage was that operators did not have

Original model for Morse's code, from Alfred Vail's notebook of 1837.

to understand the message, or even the language, that was being transmitted. They simply had to correctly interpret the signal and transcribe the characters.

The relative simplicity and ease of Morse's telegraph meant that, within a mere fifteen years, it was the standard telegraph system for most of the world, except for the British Empire, which kept the Cooke and Wheatstone system until the early twentieth century. The expansion of telegraphy and telegraph systems was extraordinarily rapid. The number of messages sent by Western Union alone was already 5.8 million in 1867, but rose to a staggering 63.2 million by 1900. When Samuel Morse died in 1872, there were more than 200,000 miles of telegraph wire across the United States alone, and much of the world was already joined by undersea cables.

Despite the extraordinary success of the Morse system, and its survival throughout the twentieth century – largely owing to its applicability for radio communications – it did not spontaneously spring into life from a mere idea. From the end of the eighteenth century onwards, many developments took place in what we would call coded communications at a distance. Flags had been used to send very simple messages between ships for centuries, and are still used today, but a means to send simple messages over long distances was needed and several systems were devised in the eighteenth century. One of the most successful was the Chappe telegraph. Designed by Claude Chappe for Napoleon's army, the Chappe telegraph was a series of line-of-sight semaphore buildings, built with a controllable beam and two arms. A code of 92 positions allowed for 8,462 coded words to be transmitted between stations. The words would be coded into combinations of the 92 positions of the arms, which would be repeated down the line to be translated with a code book at the destination. This was certainly the inspiration for Morse's first idea for sending numeric codes using a code book, or dictionary, as many such systems existed by the 1830s.

The Chappe telegraph was extremely successful – a famous abuse of the system features in Alexandre Dumas' The Count of Monte Cristo (1844) – and continued in use well into the nineteenth century. Semaphore systems for communicating with ships at sea, from port, continued until the advent of ubiquitous radio communication in the mid-twentieth century.

There were also other telegraphs in development, or even in use, in the early nineteenth century. I have already mentioned the Cooke and Wheatstone system. This was a two-dial telegraph which needed four wires, thus increasing the cost, yet the British used it throughout the empire until the end of the nineteenth century. There were also many improvements made to Morse's initial system. As the telegraph industry exploded in the mid-nineteenth century, so did the need for new and improved telegraph technology. Most of this innovation was

Workings of a Chappe
telegraph, 19th-century
engraving.

Fig. 19. — Télégraphe de Chappe.

in the form of better and more reliable batteries, but transmission and
reception devices were also improved. One area that received much
attention both in the United States and Europe was the ability to record
messages automatically.

Many histories of the telegraph and telecommunications identify
Morse's telegraph, and particularly Morse's code, as the forerunner
of digital communications. However, Morse's code is not a binary, or
digital, code. It is what we call a quinary code, as it is based on five
elements:

Cooke and Wheatstone four-dial electric telegraph.

1 short mark, dot or 'dit' (·)
2 longer mark, dash or 'dah' (–)
3 intra-character gap (between the dots and dashes within
   a character)
4 short gap (between letters)
5 medium gap (between words)

The major problem with such codes, like the Morse or even the Chappe and semaphore codes, is that they are very hard to interpret mechanically. As they need to be sent by an operator, each with their own 'hand', or style, the receiver must be equally skilled in 'reading' the transmission. There are countless stories of how telegraph operators could immediately tell who was sending a message by the rhythm of the transmission. Even today, ham radio operators, who continue to use Morse's code, recognize the rhythm of transmissions from friends.

Despite this, as early as the 1850s there were systems that sent printed messages. One of the first and most successful was the Hughes printing telegraph. Developed by David Edward Hughes, an American of Welsh decent, the Hughes printing telegraph did not use Morse's code but adopted a very different system. Hughes's telegraph utilized a piano-like keyboard (Hughes came from a very musical family and was an accomplished musician himself) with 26 keys, each corresponding to a letter of the English alphabet. The message was typed out on this keyboard by an operator and the message was then printed on paper tape at a receiving Hughes telegraph connected by wire to the sending telegraph.

This printing of messages was a great advance as it meant that not only could errors be quickly detected, but messages could be stored and sent in batches later. Storage of messages also allowed information to be archived more quickly and efficiently. In fact, the ability to store transmitted information mechanically, which the Hughes printing telegraph initiated, would be a foundational feature of telecommunications and information technologies in the future.

The Hughes printing telegraph was widely used, as Hughes sold the patent to the American Telegraph Company in 1855. The ATC was the chief rival of Western Union, and by 1864 these were the only two telegraph companies left in the U.S. ATC would go on, in the twentieth century, to develop telephones and become the American Telephone and Telegraph Company (AT&T). Despite the use and backing of one of the largest telegraph companies in the world (ATC), the Hughes system

Hughes Letter-printing Telegraph built by Siemens and Halske in St Petersburg, Russia, *c.* 1900.

had a major drawback. Both the sending and the receiving machines had to be synchronized before a transmission could commence:

> It is essential that the machines shall run at approximately the same speed, and that the type-wheels shall start from zero at the commencement of working. The former requirement is met by sending one letter, such as 'A' continuously while the receiving instrument coils are cut out for 10 revolutions. If, at the end of 10 revolutions, the signal 'A' is still printed, then the speed is sufficiently close, otherwise the governor must be regulated until this requirement is obtained.[4]

The British Post Office's manual of 1919 outlines just how hard it was to get the Hughes telegraph to send and receive messages. This used a great deal of the operator's time and did not significantly overcome the problem of operators and errors. There was also the problem that the Hughes telegraph could only send one message at a time, and the already bloated telegraph systems of the world were straining with the traffic.

So by the 1860s, the now exploding telegraph industry had few options. There was the army of Morse key coders who would expertly click out the messages, and read those dots and dashes, given rhythm by the pauses and 'hands' of senders, but this was expensive and relatively slow. It had the additional problem of error and lack of recording. The Hughes printing telegraph overcame a few problems, but came with a large set of its own: it was very slow, requiring considerable time to calibrate and then recalibrate, still requiring someone to monitor the equipment at each end. Even the Cooke and Wheatstone system, used by the British, of which we will have more to say later, provided no advantage over Morse's code. Something needed to change.

Baudot and the origin of digital codes

On 20 October 1878, Alexander Graham Bell, the first person to be awarded a patent for the telephone, was in Paris. Bell had been in England enjoying a break from the rigours of the formation of his company, the Bell Telephone Company – later to join with ATC to form AT&T – as well as a bit of a holiday with his new wife, Daisy. The formation of his company and his marriage had occurred days apart in July 1877. Bell's stay in Europe was extended due to the almost immediate pregnancy of Daisy with their first child, Elsie. Though he spent most of his time in England, Bell was in Paris that October to receive the Grande Médaille d'Or (Great Gold Medal) at the Exposition Universelle (World's Fair), for his work on the telephone.

The Paris Exposition Universelle of 1878, which ran from May to the end of October, was a very important event. Not only was it the largest World's Fair to date, drawing a staggering 13 million visitors over six months – an unheard of number at the time, especially in a city then with an estimated population of around half a million – but it was also France's attempt to re-establish itself after its crushing defeat in the Franco-Prussian War (1870–71). Devastated and humiliated as a country, France sought to regain credibility with an enormous World's Fair, one to humble all previous fairs. It was at this fair that the first bits of the – soon to be shipped to New York – Statue of Liberty were displayed, and that the purpose-built Palais du Trocadéro was opened.

These architectural emblems aside, on the night of 21 October 1878, in the Palais de l'Industrie, the French awarded Médailles for what they considered the most significant technological achievements of the age. Though it was a bittersweet moment for Bell, as he had to share the accolade with both Elisha Gray and Thomas Edison – Edison also getting a prize for the phonograph – it demonstrated the importance that the new French Third Republic placed on telecommunications. Though history continues to flatter these two American, and one British, pioneers of the telephone, others received medals that night for advances in telecommunications. Now largely forgotten – except by a few historians and, strangely, ham radio operators – a Frenchman, Jean-Maurice-Émile Baudot, also received a Grande Médaille d'Or that night for what was to become one of the most significant inventions not of the nineteenth century, but for the twentieth century.

Émile Baudot was born in eastern France, the son of local farmers. Though he had only an elementary education, finding that he was not that interested in farming, Baudot joined the French Post & Telegraph Administration (Administration des Postes et Télégraphes) in 1869, at the age of 24.[5] The Post & Telegraph Administration trained the young Baudot in both Morse's code and the Hughes printing telegraph. Baudot was conscripted into the army for the disastrous war against Prussia, but returned to his duties with the Post & Telegraph Administration in Paris in 1872. From the fall of Paris to that date, it seems that the young Baudot had started working on a better way to transmit messages as telegrams.

At the time that Baudot joined the Post & Telegraph Administration, there were only two types of direct transmission telegraphs in use:

the Cooke and Wheatstone telegraph and the Morse. The Cooke and Wheatstone telegraph was a strange device that drew its inspiration from the much older semaphore systems, having one, two or five needles that were deflected either to the right or left to signify different characters. Much more complicated, and much slower, than the Morse telegraph, it not surprisingly failed to find favour with the rest of the world, which opted for Morse's system. However, the British Empire was vast, covering almost one-third of the globe, and needed to be communicated with. So most telegraph companies also had Cooke and Wheatstone telegraphs for communication with Britain and its Empire.

In France, though, the Morse telegraph was the dominant system used by the Post & Telegraph Administration, so this was the first telegraph system that the young Baudot used. He was also trained in the Hughes printing telegraph (1855). One problem with the Morse telegraph, and its code, was that it was difficult and somewhat slow to transcribe. Though, with skill, operators could process Morse code much faster than Cooke and Wheatstone code, it remained a difficult process. Many devices were designed in the mid-nineteenth century to record or print Morse's code, but the dominant one was that of David Edward Hughes.

Having a phenomenal capacity for work, the young Baudot quickly realized that these systems had many drawbacks and that improvements were needed if telegraphy was to grow. He was not alone in this realization, as the end of the nineteenth century saw a vast number of inventions and improvements to telegraphy. However, Baudot would take telecommunications in a very different direction.

Through those difficult years immediately after the Franco-Prussian War, Baudot worked, in his own time and with his own resources, not just to improve existing telegraphs, but to transform them. Other telegraphs, such as Hughes's, were not much more than Morse modems, and Baudot saw the fundamental problems with message transmission. These were (1) the very slow transmission rates and (2) the unreliable transmission and reception of the message characters.

What Baudot did was to transform both the machinery for transmission and the code.

Baudot's Printing Telegraph, which he patented in 1874, was what we would today call a 'synchronous time division multiplex system'. Not only could it send up to six messages down the same wire at the same time, what is called multiplex, but it could do so *synchronously*, in a steady continuous stream. What this means is that, whereas the other systems, such as Morse's or the Cooke and Wheatstone, would send characters of different lengths distinguished by a short gap – asynchronously – Baudot's system sent characters in a synchronized stream as each character code was exactly the same length and had exactly the same number of elements. Though, like all inventions, Baudot's mechanism and code was the application and improvement of earlier innovations, he was the first to put these bits together. Most significant for us is that Baudot was the first to recognize the importance of a simple 5-bit binary code – a digital code.

Binary, or quasi-binary, codes had been developed before; the most notable was that of Carl Friedrich Gauss and Wilhelm Weber as of 1834. However, none of these earlier binary codes was digital. The reason that they could be binary, but not digital, was that though they were a code comprised of just two states, each letter encoding could comprise anything from one to four bits, much like Morse's code. What distinguished Baudot's code and, as we shall see, offered such enormous potential for encoding just about anything, was its constant length. The Baudot code was a 5-bit binary code, and all binary communications, and computer information, is still encoded by fixed-length binary code – digital code.

Baudot's printing telegraph, his actual apparatus, was a strange mechanism that used a piano-style five-key keypad, which was operated with two fingers of the left hand and three of the right hand. Operators had to learn the code for each letter and number, and enter these in a steady rhythm to keep up with the transmission. Baudot's operators are the vast number of workers who could read digital code to whom I referred in the Introduction. To add to the complexity,

Baudot's code, as a 5-bit code, could only encode 32 characters. This is not enough for the letters of the Latin alphabet and the numerals. There was also a need to encode certain 'control characters' such as a carriage return or a line feed. To solve this problem, Baudot introduced a 'shift character'. When the code 01000^6 was transmitted, the receiving device changed register and the following codes printed a *shift* set of letters, numerals and control codes. If another 01000 was

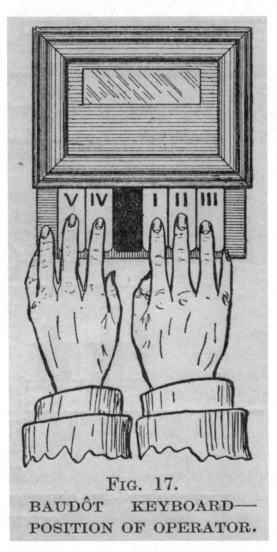

Baudot's five-key keypad for direct entry of 5-bit digital codes, from the 1870s.

FIG. 17.
BAUDÔT KEYBOARD—
POSITION OF OPERATOR.

Letters	Figures	KEYS					Letters	Figures	KEYS				
		V	IV	I	II	III			V	IV	I	II	III
A	1			◍			P	+	◍	◍	◍	◍	◍
B	8		◍			◍	Q	/	◍	◍	◍		◍
C	9		◍	◍		◍	R	−	◍	◍			◍
D	0		◍	◍	◍	◍	S	7	◍				◍
E	2				◍		T	2	◍		◍		◍
F	5		◍		◍	◍	U	4			◍		◍
G	7		◍		◍		V	'	◍		◍	◍	◍
H	1		◍	◍	◍		W	?	◍			◍	◍
I	3/				◍	◍	X	9	◍			◍	
J	6		◍	◍			Y	3					◍
K	(	◍	◍	◍			Z	:	◍		◍	◍	
L	=	◍	◍	◍	◍		−	.	◍		◍		
M	)	◍	◍		◍		✻	✻	◍	◍	[Erasure]		
N	£	◍	◍		◍	◍	Figure & space	shift		◍			
O	5			◍	◍	◍	Letter & space	shift	◍				
/	7/			◍	◍								

FIG. 22.

BAUDÔT SIGNALLING CODE OR ALPHABET (BRITISH).

Baudot's 5-bit code, from Pendry's monograph of 1919.

then received, the character register would shift back, allowing for a full 64 characters to be transmitted. This was much like the typewriter shift key or our own shift or control keys on the computer keyboard, where the characters change when pressed and change back when released.

As a printing telegraph, using a synchronous code, a further innovation of Baudot's telegraph was that it punched the digital code onto a continuous paper tape at both ends – both on the transmitting telegraph and on the receiving telegraph. The first version did not print characters, but, like all the other printing telegraphs, except Hughes's, it punched the digital codes directly onto a paper tape. This form of printing digital continued well into the twentieth century, and digital punched tape was one of the first recording media used for electronic computers in the 1940s and '50s.

A punched tape was very useful for several reasons. First, as operators could read the codes, as they had to type them directly into the telegraph, they could also read the tape. This provided a means for storing messages to be either transmitted or even written out at a later time, thus increasing efficiency. Second, since a punched tape could store a message, if messages needed to be sent on from one station to another, the tape could simply be fed into a transmitter rather than recoded, thus decreasing error. Mostly, though, this meant that accurate recording of messages could be stored for later reference and use, exist as multiple copies and be processed back into letters on multiple devices – but more of this quality of the digital later.

Baudot's Printing Telegraph could achieve a rate of about thirty words per minute, much faster than other printing telegraphs of the time. As a result, the Baudot telegraph would be used for various purposes throughout the world for over seventy years. Though Baudot's mechanism was both innovative and effective, and was used for several high-capacity routes, it was never very popular. The reasons for this were many, but primarily Baudot's telegraph and code came at a time when other systems had already been widely adopted. The enormous investment in the Cooke and Wheatstone telegraph and the Morse telegraph meant that, despite their drawbacks, improvements to these systems were more economical than wholesale replacement. This was reflected in the slow but steady uptake of Baudot's system. It was almost immediately accepted for limited use by the French in 1875, and a line using Baudot's telegraph was opened between Paris and Rome by the end of 1877. It was then progressively introduced in France, but never as the dominant system. Other countries in Europe saw its utility and introduced it more extensively. Italy first introduced it in 1887 for all in-country telegraphs, and the Netherlands, Switzerland, Austria and Brazil introduced Baudot telegraphs by the end of the century. Even the British Post Office adopted it for a single circuit between London and Paris in 1897.

Another major drawback of Baudot's telegraph was that it required the operator to directly enter the digital code for each letter. Though, with skill, this was a much more efficient system than Morse's, it was difficult to learn and the skills could not be used on other machines. Though Baudot improved his system throughout his life (he died in 1903), even funding his work by selling his Grande Médaille d'Or, these problems were not resolved until the beginning of the twentieth century, not by Baudot but by a New Zealand newspaper reporter, Donald Murray.

Throughout the latter half of the nineteenth century, office technologies had also been growing rapidly. Many of the office technologies that we take for granted today were developed at this time, such as the card index, the vertical file with its file folders and tabs, which is the foundation of our laptop file-systems. But another technology that is pervasive today was being developed: the typewriter keypad. We don't use typewriters much today, though I did in my youth, but we do all type using a keyboard – a keyboard that was developed in the early twentieth century for typewriters.

The first typewriters were developed in the early and mid-nineteenth century, but although the design that we are used to took shape during this time, none was ever mass-produced. It was not until the early 1870s, when Baudot was just finishing his telegraph and code, that three Americans – Christopher Latham Sholes, Carlos Glidden and Samuel W. Soule – finally delivered their prototype typewriter to their backers, James Densmore and George Washington Newton Yost. Densmore and Yost would, in 1873, strike a deal with the successful sewing machine manufacturer E. Remington & Sons to manufacture the first commercially available typewriter. Remington would go on to be a dominant force in typewriters and office machinery,[7] the new typewriter would quickly become an important instrument in all offices, especially in newspapers, and it was a young newspaper journalist who would find a new use for the typewriter – attach it to a telegraph.

Why exactly the young Donald Murray, that young New Zealand newspaper journalist, and hence someone who was well versed in the

use of typewriters, should turn his attention to improving the telegraph remains unknown. Though Murray wrote extensively, he never
gave a clue as to why he would change careers and, in 1898, leave
New Zealand for New York to patent and manufacture a new type of
telegraph. In Murray's paper of 1905, 'Setting Type by Telegraph', he
describes his innovation of combining the typewriter keyboard with a
telegraph. Of course, Hughes and Baudot had used keyboards before,
but only as a synchronized printing system, and not typewriter keyboards. What Murray did was to combine, and improve, the Baudot
telegraph and its digital code with a typewriter. Murray also chose
the dominant typewriter keyboard in use from the first Remington
typewriter – the QWERTY keyboard.

Over the preceding thirty years, there had been a developing crisis in
telegraphy, as use had exploded but transmission remained relatively
slow. At the same time, there had been an explosion in the number
of skilled typists, in line with the phenomenal uptake of typewriters
for all forms of information recording and business correspondence.
Even in telecommunications, telegraphs, sent by whatever method,

Donald Murray's telegraph with a QWERTY keyboard.

were, by the end of century, invariably typed out for delivery using the new typewriter.

What Donald Murray did was to combine these two common processes, and technologies, into one telegraph. Adopting some of Baudot's mechanism, as well as his digital code, meant that Murray's telegraph could exploit all the advantages of speed, storage and accuracy that the Baudot system offered. However, by replacing Baudot's abstruse keyboard with a QWERTY typewriter keyboard, characters could simply be typed directly into the telegraph, which would transmit them as digital code and print out not digital code at the other end, but characters. By combining these two pervasive technologies, Murray created one of the most powerful communication technologies of the twentieth century – the direct machine encoding of information.

As the system did not require the operator to directly enter the digital codes, Murray could optimize Baudot's digital character code so as to minimize wear and tear on the transmission and printing machines. This was the first in a long line of transformations of Baudot's original digital code. Sticking with the 5-bit encoding, Murray reassigned some of the codes for the most common characters in English. Murray also added further control characters such as the NULL or BLANK and DEL codes. The NULL/BLANK code (00000) would be used to tell the receiving machine to wait, while DEL would tell the receiving telegraph to delete the previous character.

Murray's system separated, forever, the operator from the code. Whereas with all previous character codes, operators directly entered the code for characters and 'read' the received *code*, with the Murray system, operators did not have to have any understanding of the code at all. As with our own laptops and mobiles, which use a digital encoding almost identical to Murray's, at least for the basic Latin letters that we enter, we do not enter or read digital codes, but type letters and numbers. We let the machine sort out the digital encoding, processing and their translation back into characters and numbers. What Murray did, probably unwittingly, was to establish one of the key qualities of digital encoding: the separation of the digital code from its referent.

While there was no direct relationship between Baudot's code and the letters and numbers they signified, like letters they could be read by the skilled. Murray made this relationship redundant in digital encoding, burying the encoding within the infrastructure of the machine itself, thus making digital encoding non-representational.

From keyed to digital telegraphs

By the beginning of the twentieth century, the limitations of the now international telegraph systems based on either the Wheatstone–Creed or Morse systems were becoming too obvious to be ignored. The telegraph systems, which created a global communications system, were now too cumbersome to accommodate its phenomenal growth. The piecemeal development of, and replacement of asynchronous telegraph systems with, systems based on the Baudot–Murray digital code were growing, but it was clear by the second decade of the twentieth century that something more radical had to be done.

The impetus came from the Postmaster General of Great Britain, Herbert L. Samuel, who, in 1913, formed a committee to inquire into the potential of high-speed telegraphs. The brief of the committee, which met eight times between 1913 and 1914, was to examine both Morse and non-Morse systems for both cost and efficiency. Considering only those existing telegraph technologies in use outside the United States, the 'high-speed committee' inquired specifically into four issues: the comparative efficiency and costs of multiplex systems and 'automatic' printing systems; improvements to the use of a type-keyboard; the utility of Baudot digital encoding as opposed to Morse's code; and the relative merits of full page printing and paper tape or slip printing.

The committee delivered its initial findings in 1914, and the full report was published in 1916.[8] The conclusions were definitive. The committee concluded:

The Wheatstone system, even with the addition of the Creed accessories, is not considered by the committee as suitable for commercial telegraph work . . . [T]he correction of errors becomes a matter of considerable difficulty.[9]

This decision by one of the largest postal services in the world, the Postal Service of Great Britain, which ran all the British telegraph services throughout the British Empire, sounded the death knell of the Wheatstone–Creed system, but also of the Morse system for use in telegraphs. The advantages of digital codes and digital transmission systems were clear. The ability to send multiplex, synchronous code between machines where operators could simply type in the messages using a keyboard, and the message could then be printed out as characters at the other end, transformed telecommunications after the First World War. Interestingly, Morse's code found a new lease of life for transmission of messages via the new technology of radio. The impossibility of machine encoding of any sort on radio, until the 1960s, and the high energy demands for clear transmission of voice by radio, meant that Morse's code would remain in use well into the twentieth century, but not for telegraphs and telegrams.

A digital world: teleprinting and telex

it [will] not be long ere the whole surface of this country [is] channelled for those nerves which are to diffuse, with the speed of thought, a knowledge of all that is occurring throughout the land.

SAMUEL MORSE, 1838[10]

The end of the nineteenth and beginning of the twentieth centuries saw a phenomenal growth in communications technologies and in the extent of international coverage. Most rural areas in all parts of the world had some access to telegraphs, while telephone use was also expanding rapidly by the 1920s. Such a level of growth in telecommunications would not be repeated until the growth in mobile telephone use at the beginning of the twenty-first century. The shift from the cumbersome and expensive telegraph systems of Morse and Wheatstone and Creed to vastly more efficient digital systems meant that telegraph was no longer the exclusive preserve of the rich, corporations or governments. Telegrams were fast becoming a means for quick and simple communication. Though not mobile or immediate, as with SMS today, by mid-century people would often send a telegram if they were delayed on the train, or needed to get news to someone quickly. Because of the possibilities for automation opened up by the shift to digital technologies, costs were falling and volume was on the increase.

The possibility of automation was quickly realized, and in 1924 AT&T introduced a new fully integrated printing telegraph with a typewriter keyboard. The new system, called teletype – or teleprinters in Europe – used the Baudot–Murray code, and sent the digital signal as electric impulses. As with the Murray system, an operator at one teletype would type in the message while connected to another teletype somewhere else in the world via the telephone system. The message would automatically print out, onto paper, on the other teletype. The advantage of teletype was that it could not only send messages to one other machine, but any number of receiving teletypes, thus introducing the use of digitally encoded messages for fast dissemination of news.

Teletype, telex and teleprinters dominated inter-office and intergovernmental printed communications until the advent of the fax in the 1970s and '80s. Using the Baudot code, by the 1930s internationally standardized as the ITA2 code, teleprinting became the dominant form of information transmission, especially between offices or governmental departments, throughout the twentieth century. The fact that, in the 1950s, there was a well-established technology for typing and printing digitally encoded text and numerals meant that teleprinters were quickly adopted as the predominant means for typing instructions into the new digital computers, as well as printing the output.

Though I will discuss this relationship between teleprinters and digital computers later, this brief aside into teleprinting is to show how this shift to digitally encoded telecommunications at the beginning of the twentieth century laid the foundations for digitally encoded communication with computers in the 1950s.

2
DATA ENCODING AND STORAGE BEFORE THE COMPUTER

Detaching the operators from the process of encoding/decoding and transmission – by being able to store messages on a paper tape and then reproduce it exactly, digitally – was a key factor in the ultimate success of Baudot's system. Digital encoding allowed for a simple and accurate encoding that machines could decipher and process. Because encoding and decoding of digital messages could be mechanized, the Baudot–Murray code became the only mechanized encoding of telegraph messages by the 1920s. This chapter explores the many transformations that Baudot's code underwent throughout the twentieth century, and how the new technologies of copying and storing impacted the development of the digital.

The digital was not only solving problems of data transmission, of telegraphy, but a critical feature of digital encoding in data communications was the ability to print and store data. Storing messages, whether for retransmission or just for a record, was a primary consideration of the Baudot system. This chapter will also explore how another problem was resolved through the use of the digital: the problem of message duplication and storage, or copying. Copying messages while they were being entered, mechanically, and again when they were received, ensured much greater accuracy and volume, but mostly allowed for their duplication and storage. It was the humble process of copying that transformed information recording and transmission from individual products into a mass medium.

One of the key problems of message transmission is to ensure that a message sent is the same at both ends – from the point of transmission and at the point of reception. It seems trivial today that if we send a message, an email or an SMS, what we write will arrive at the other end as we wrote it. However, this was a huge problem in the early days of the telegraph and telecommunications. Even with the early telephone, there was a huge problem with simply *being heard*. With the advent of Morse's telegraph, there was a great deal of attention given to the skills of the telegraph operators to ensure, as much as possible, that they encoded the message correctly and that they could correctly 'read' a message. This was no simple skill, as while encoding could easily be learned, 'reading' a message was very much harder. It was not simply a matter of decoding a series of dots and dashes, but interpreting a series of dots and dashes, sent differently by different hands, and often weak or obscured due to problems or noise on the line. A great deal of time was lost by the telegraph operators simply clarifying and retransmitting messages.

Even today, much of the work done by the Internet is merely checking that the data sent is the same at both ends – though this is done automatically within, and between, servers. On the Internet this error checking ensures absolute fidelity between the sent and received messages. However, fidelity of the message remained a major problem for all data transmission well into the twentieth century. From the earliest days of the telegraph, in the 1840s, to the advent of reliable digital communications at the beginning of the twentieth century, the need to ensure the message was the same at both ends not only generated a large number of technical solutions, but brought about the emergence of a number of unforeseen advantages and consequences.

The same at both ends, regardless of the mechanism

At the end of the nineteenth century, one of the most important considerations for the exploding telegraphy industry was the cost of transmission. As we discussed in the previous chapter, telegraphy used a variety of mechanisms to send text over wire. From the 1850s, though the Hughes telegraph allowed accurate transmission and accurate duplication at the receiving, it required a great deal of effort to ensure accurate transmission and reception. It required that operators continuously monitor, calibrate and synchronize devices at both ends before, during and after transmission, and could only create one copy by this process.

To review the situation, with Morse's code, the operator ensured accuracy by keying the code directly and another operator listened to the dots and dashes and wrote down the message. This was slow and required many operators, but did not require any calibration or synchronization of the devices, and the key operators were very reliable. If a message had to be sent some distance, you would need to send it 'down the line', which meant that one operator would key the message to the next nearest operator, who would write the message down. Then the second operator would key the message to the next operator down the line, and so forth. This form of electrical 'broken telephone' not only required lots of operators and was slow and expensive, but was prone to many errors.[1] Error correction was very easy, albeit very slow, simply a matter of the operators checking with each other that the message was correct.

The Cooke and Wheatstone system, used extensively in Britain and throughout the British Empire, used a series of dials and could send a message over long distances. However, this too needed operators at both ends, transmitting and receiving, and was prone to the same sorts of operator error. The Baudot system, though not yet common at the end of the nineteenth century, was prone to operator fatigue as the keying had to be done in cadence with the transmitting mechanism. So, by the end of the nineteenth century, there was a recognition by the telegraph companies that something needed to be done if they were to continue to grow and for costs to come down. The ideal solution was to introduce a mechanism that would record the message directly from the transmitted signal.

Numerous printing systems were invented during the nineteenth century, but very few were ever put into general use, as operators remained both sufficiently accurate and relatively cheap. For example, in 1841, Charles Wheatstone, the co-inventor of the Cooke–Wheatstone telegraph, built a device for use on his and William Cooke's telegraph that would print out the message. Wheatstone used an electromagnetically operated hammer that struck a letter-printing type mounted on the spoke of a wheel, which very much resembled the daisy-wheel printer so common in the 1970s and '80s. Though functional, this mechanism was very slow, so proved to be not very effective. More pervasive was Edward Calahan's 'stock ticker', a simple mechanical device which printed letters, transmitted directly by wire from the stock exchange, onto paper tape. The vast quantity of paper tape generated by these devices in businesses and in the stock exchange is what gave rise to the famous ticker-tape parades in New York.

There were many other printing devices available. There were the printers of Bréguet and Siemens & Halske, which were widely used in Russia and central Europe. There was the Bain printer and Steinheil's recording telegraph. Charles Wheatstone went on to create another, more successful, printer for inscribing and printing Morse code, the Wheatstone automatic high-speed recorder. Wheatstone also made a transmitter that used 'double current' – current in one direction for the dots and dashes, and a reverse current for the gaps in between – thereby vastly improving the accuracy of the transmission. The most successful of the automatic telegraphs was Wheatstone's transmitter, and his later improved high-speed recorders, some of which remained in service with the British Post Office up to the 1930s. However, none of these automatic telegraphs gained general acceptance, as, in the nineteenth century, costs of operators were generally low, especially in the 'colonies', so there was little economic incentive to introduce new and costly equipment.

As discussed previously, a 'high-speed committee' formed by the British Postmaster General to transform and standardize British telegraphy met just before the First World War. This was a significant development not only because it recognized the need for standardization of code as the key to high-speed telegraphy, but also because, coming as it did from the British Postmaster General, developments in Britain would affect the rest of the world. The committee started its work in 1913, but did not finish until 1916 due to the enormity of the task and the pressing demands of the war. However, when it did report, the conclusions were definitive. The committee offered four conclusions:

1 multiplex systems offered a clear advantage over merely automatic systems
2 there was a clear and unassailable advantage to a full typewriter keyboard system over single or multiple key systems
3 the Baudot code was clearly preferable to the Morse code
4 complete page printing was preferable to printed tape or slips, even if these were gummed for pasting onto a single page.

Of the seventeen different systems reviewed, including Morse's code, perforator systems, dial systems and keyboard and key entry systems, they rejected all but one, the Baudot–Murray system. Thus the stage was set for a transformation of telecommunications, at least for text transmission, from diverse codes to a single international digital code.

Data entry and print codes: ITA, FIELDATA and ASCII

The digital character code created by Baudot in the 1870s has dominated, or fundamentally influenced, character encoding up to the present day. Though the character encoding that we use today on all of our digital devices, mostly Unicode, is vast compared to Baudot's code, accommodating as it does today almost all the languages of the world, and many languages now long dead, the encoding of the Latin letters and the numerals is essentially the same as that of the Baudot–Murray code. It is an interesting set of developments, tangents, dead ends and circumstances that have led to today's character codes, but they all start with Baudot.

Throughout the later nineteenth century, given that there was already a skilled workforce of operators and technicians dedicated to these established systems of encoding and transmission, there was little impetus for governments or telegraph companies to change. However, by the early twentieth century the need for a more effective, standard and mechanized encoding was seen as imperative and it was Baudot's code that won out. By this time, though, even Baudot's code was feeling the strain of having to accommodate new technologies.

One of the first limitations of Baudot's original encoding, which became apparent as soon as Donald Murray adapted the new typewriter keyboard to a Baudot encoder and transmitter, was the efficiency of the encoding for individual letters. You may ask, sensibly, why would the actual pattern of holes and non-holes in a 5-bit digital code make any difference regardless of how you were entering the letters and numbers? Today, with electronic storage, processing and transmission, the actual pattern of bits in the encoding hardly matters. If you are entering, storing, processing and transmitting 5 digital bits, it is not that relevant to the computer which of those bits are ons and which are offs, as long as the encoding is consistent. However, at the turn of the twentieth century, when these encodings and their transmission, reception and processing were all mechanical, or electromechanical, the actual pattern of holes and non-holes did matter because it meant more or less work for the mechanical parts of the machinery. More mechanical work not only meant more maintenance, and more frequent part replacement, but slower transmission speeds. When Baudot began his work, these impacts on maintenance and speed were not very significant as his system was as reliable and cost-effective as many others, and he could then achieve higher speeds. However, by the turn of the century, with the growing volume of telegraph traffic, these impacts mattered a great deal. This is the main reason why Donald Murray not only coupled a typewriter keyboard with a Baudot encoder and transmitter, but altered Baudot's original code.

This was especially important as Murray's system did not directly transmit the encoded message; instead his keyboard encoder punched the 5-bit code onto a paper tape as the operator 'struck' the typewriter keys. The paper tape, with the message code punched onto it, was then fed into a tape transmitter where, at the receiving end, the encoded message was either printed out, letter by letter, with the holes, onto another paper tape, or another perforated paper tape was made using a 'reperforator', for storage or later transmission. These electromechanical devices suffered a lot of wear and tear from these perforation and printing actions. Also, the operators typing in the message needed to do so efficiently and with minimum effort. An efficient pattern of digital encoding was therefore of primary concern to Murray. Thus Murray's code differs from Baudot's by giving the most frequently used letters, in English, the smallest number of holes, hence the smallest amount of punching on the paper tape. For example, the letters E and T, the space and the carriage and line feeds all had only one 'hole' in their encoding in Murray's code. However, as Murray's code retained the 5-bit encoding, and was largely the same as Baudot's, it is still often referred to as the Baudot–Murray code.

One frequently asked question is why, if a 5-bit code could only accommodate 32 elements (32 letters, numbers and punctuation characters), did Baudot use a 5-bit code, and why did Murray keep it? Of course, 32 elements weren't sufficient for Baudot, so he used a shift code to get up to 64 elements, thus accommodating all the capital Latin characters, a space, the ten digits, a number of punctuation marks and some extra necessary control characters. But why did Baudot not simply go for a 6-bit code that would allow for 64 elements in the first place, or even a 7-bit code that would allow 128 elements? The answer is down to the technology available at the time. Well into the twentieth century, an electromechanical device to encode and decode a 6-bit character code was an order of magnitude more complex than the one devised by Baudot. Baudot simply could not effectively build such a device in the 1870s, and it remained next to impossible to effectively and economically build such a device until the 1940s. Thus the 5-bit code remained the standard, whatever its patterns, well into the mid-twentieth century.

The success of the 5-bit Baudot–Murray code was ensured not only by the adoption of the encoding and its telegraph systems by the British Post Office in 1916, but also by the fact that, earlier, in April 1912, Murray sold both his patents, and hence the use of his code, to the Western Union Telegraph Company of the United States. With the acceptance of Baudot–Murray's encoding and transmission system, or a variant of it, by both the British Post Office and one of the largest telegraph companies in the U.S. by 1916, rather than stability, many variants of 5-bit character codes began to appear. Not only was there Baudot–Murray's encoding, but that of others, such as Frederick Creed, who created competing versions of Baudot's code. The British Post Office used mostly Creed's version, while Western Union worked on further developing systems that advanced on Murray's original patents, also further modifying and adding to the code. Joy Morton, the owner of the American company Morton Salt, also entered the industry with the Morkrum company, which had its own machinery and its own 5-bit code.

International Telegraph Alphabet No. 2 (ITA2) standard

By the mid-1920s there were any number of 5-bit digital codes, or variants of digital codes, in operation around the world. In France, they still used both Baudot's equipment and his code, Murray's variation was used in many places, and there were many variations of Murray's code. There were national versions of the 5-bit code, as well as different language versions – or at least different versions for different alphabets such as Cyrillic or Greek. The confusion caused by different ways of sending telegraph messages had been quickly replaced by a cacophony of diverse 5-bit digital codes. Many, including Donald Murray and A. E. Thompson, as well as the Germans, had been pressing for some standardization from as early as 1921. By the mid-1920s most agreed that something had to be done.

In 1926, the Bureau International de l'Union Télégraphique had reformed into a much larger organization, the Comité Consultatif International Télégraphiques (CCIT). The Bureau International de l'Union Télégraphique was the organization that had standardized Morse's code decades earlier, after a similar multiplication of versions of Morse's code had caused major problems for the telegraph industry. At the first meeting of the new CCIT held in November 1926, in Berlin, the main item on the agenda was a standardized 5-bit digital code. Another agenda item was to devise a standardized measure of transmission speed, which was defined as the number of digital bits per second and named the baud in honour of Baudot. A baud was designated by digital bits, in contrast to the calculation of transmission speeds for analogue signals, which have many more variables and are much more complicated. We still use baud rates today to measure digital transmission speeds.

However, the main business of the CCIT was a standardized digital code. There was much discussion, and even more disagreement, with the French arguing that the code had to be Baudot's, or something very close to it, as their operators could not be compelled to learn a new code. Despite this intransigence, or perhaps because of it, a technical subcommittee was appointed and concluded that the new standardized code would have to be a variant of Baudot's original.[2]

This resolved, inevitably more arguments broke out about exactly what variations were needed. The British wanted a clear use of letter space and figure space characters, while the USSR sought to keep the separate shift registers as they had too many letters for one shift register. The Czechs wanted the Comité to address the problem of accented characters, while Frederick Creed wished the CCIT to consider a 6-bit code. Needless to say, the first meeting of the CCIT adjourned without reaching a consensus.

During the intervening years before the next CCIT meeting, to be held in June 1929, many of the conflicts were negotiated through and solutions devised. So at the second meeting of the CCIT in June 1929, also held in Berlin, a solution for the standard 5-bit, Baudot-derived code could be presented – the International Telegraph Alphabet No. 1 (ITA1). As a result of this apparent consent forged from years of work, there was immediate conflict. The main problem was that though the proposed code may have been useful for a number of reasons, it did not map well onto the QWERTY keyboard, the typewriter keyboard most in use then, and the one most of the English-speaking world continues to use today on our computers, laptops, mobiles and pads. Suggestions were made for new keyboards, or for the possibility of complicated mechanical means to transmit the new code. However, in the session of the meeting held on 11 June the attendees reaffirmed that they preferred the direct association of Baudot–Murray's code with the keyboards and that Baudot's code should be adapted as little as possible. After the session took a break from midday to 2.15 p.m., a Dutch delegate suggested that a subcommittee investigate the best code for the then common start–stop telegraph equipment. The sub-committee was duly formed and met from 3.20 to 5.50 p.m. It returned to the meeting at 6 p.m. with a code.

The proposed code, which was adopted as the International Telegraph Alphabet No. 2 (ITA2), was basically a combination of Baudot's and Murray's letters and figures, with four positions reserved for specific national use. They additionally swapped the code for the letter P with the error character so that if a letter was printed in error the machine could backspace and punch all holes (11111) to show an error.

Now, the CCIT meeting had not one but two standardized codes on the table. The idea of having two standardized international tele-graph alphabets (ITA1 and ITA2) was strongly opposed, primarily by the USSR. To add to the complications, at a later meeting on 21 January 1931 the British announced that they would be introducing a U.S.-style teletypewriter service using Western Union's Murray-derived stand-ard, the American Teletypewriter code (USTTY). This left the CCIT with very little option but to adopt a slightly modified version of the USTTY for the ITA2 standard. At last, though, the world had a more or less standard digital code for telegraph, based on the Baudot–Murray code.

Following this consolidation, all digital character codes would be a derivative of the Baudot–Murray codes; well, not quite all – but more of this later.

Though the standardization of teletypewriter codes (ITA2 and USTTY) offered a more or less stable situation for the telegraph industry, the explosion of information processing and sharing that came with the Second World War made the limitations of a 5-bit character code extremely apparent. This was less of a problem for the telegraph industry, who only had to consistently send upper-case characters, numbers and some punctuation. For this, a 5-bit code was sufficient. However, for the military, who needed to send more data and more detailed data, the 5-bit code was proving insufficient. In the 1950s, the U.S. Army Signal Corps began developing a much expanded character code for the sole use of the military – FIELDATA.

FIELDATA

By the 1950s there was one context, the military one, in which an extended digital character encoding was desperately needed. By 'the military' we mean primarily the U.S. military, but also what emerged as NATO after the Second World War. Other militaries, the Soviet and the Chinese, used different systems, though both had telegraph systems largely based on the Baudot–Murray digital code. Not only did the Western military alliance have a variety of different communications systems and a diversity of data storage systems – systems that stored character-based information mostly on punched cards – but it was also one of the largest users of digital data. By the early 1950s it was clear that a standardized character encoding was needed to join up all the different communications and data systems of the U.S. military complex. What emerged was FIELDATA.

The computers of the time worked on a 6-bit encoding: the Baudot–Murray 5-bit code (ITA2) and one control bit. They had memory registers of 18 or 36 bits to explicitly accommodate this character encoding. So FIELDATA was essentially a 6-bit code, but it operated by using a 'tag bit' that would designate the use of one of four 'rows' of characters or supervisory codes. So, with this additional bit, FIELDATA was effectively a 7-bit code.

It is important to realize that, unlike today, in the 1950s, and even the 1960s, processing input and output of characters or numbers that were readable by humans was not something that the computer did. Computers were far too expensive, and their operation even more so, to spend time encoding digital characters, or decoding them back for the output. This was all done by other mechanisms, often mechanical or electromechanical devices, offline – basically reading the output tapes or cards from the computer and changing the digital codes into characters and printing them, or taking keyboard input and transferring the digital codes onto tapes. It was computing systems of this sort that FIELDATA was designed to deal with, to standardize the encoding into and out of computers.

With FIELDATA, data could be collected from, or sent to, any number of systems and sources. As with the digital encoding of telegraphs, where, from the early twentieth century, the transmission and reception devices could be very different, the military in the 1950s increasingly needed to be sure that if data or communications were created in one place, they could be read, transmitted, stored and/or processed in any number of other places, and on any number of other devices, as needed. This was, and is, a powerful quality of digital encoding: the ability to store and move encoded information between different devices as long as the devices agree on the structure of the code. FIELDATA could operate at these different scales, from the basic input and output devices attached to local printers, transmitters or processors, to the extremely large regional, or 'battle theatre', data processing centres.

For the first time, and for the basic need of connecting diverse mechanisms for storage, transmission and processing, a digital character code was developed that would allow character-based information to flow between all these systems and be used for a diversity of purposes. FIELDATA was the first encoding that was explicitly designed for a whole new way of processing, storing and using information, what today we would call 'integrated systems'. Today, of course, all our systems are 'integrated'. We also share a greater variety of digital data than just characters. As we will see in the next chapter, the ability of digital data to reproduce, or simulate, any medium was anticipated as early as the 1940s, but the implications of this took time to be realized. In the 1950s, though, it was quickly realized that the power of digital encoding was that it could integrate all data across all systems.

Unlike in the first half of the twentieth century, when different systems handled data differently and through different encodings, and when the movement of data from one system to another was managed by humans recoding the data, or through hand-operated mechanical transcription systems, from the 1950s onwards there was a growing sense that all these systems could be joined together by simply ensuring that the way the information was encoded was the same, and that all the mechanisms used this conventional encoding. As with the rise of the Baudot–Murray code for telegraphs, the power of FIELDATA was that it could be read, transmitted, stored and processed by any system that could read and write the code. Not only this, but the way that FIELDATA encoded characters would have a profound influence on the digital encodings that we still use today.

An aside on punching holes in paper

For both the Hughes printing telegraph and the Baudot digital telegraph, the storage of the code was a major advance. Both systems, as we discovered previously, were created to overcome a number of problems with the Morse telegraph. One in particular was that it was very hard to record and print Morse's code. In contrast, recording and printing of digital code was simple, and the preferred method of recording was ticker tape.

Ticker tape had been developed for use with the first printing telegraph built by Royal Earl House (this was his name, not his company), an American inventor, in 1846. House's early system was very unreliable, though it did introduce the principle of punching paper tape with holes that could stand for code entities. Though this punched paper tape did rely on what is often called a binary system – on or 1 when the hole was punched, and off or 0 when it was not – in fact, for the history of punched paper tape, and as we will see with punched cards, only the Baudot system was truly digital.

The reason that these earlier recording telegraphs were not digital was not only because the code was not digital, as with Morse's code, but because the punches on the tape were always there to record a code point. With a binary system such as Baudot's, both the presence and absence of a hole are code points. This is what makes the system simple two-state digital. This is an important distinction because, as we will see next, there was a great deal of punching of tape, cards and other paper documents, little of which was digital.

The Jacquard weaving loom is often cited as the origin of these punched hole technologies (see p. 59), but is also claimed as the source of all digital encoding. This origin myth, and it is largely a myth, arose due to the association of the Jacquard loom's punched pattern cards with Herman Hollerith's first punched cards for the 1890 U.S. Census, but also with their association, via the famous Ada Lovelace, with Charles Babbage's first mechanical calculator – the Difference Engine, begun in the 1820s and never finished. However, this enormous rise in punching holes was largely due to the fact that both business and government were recording ever more information about people and practices. As a result, not only documentary records, but punched cards and tape, were increasingly found everywhere.

Augusta Ada King, the Countess Lovelace, was Lord Byron's only legitimate child but was raised by her mother, having not seen her father since she was one month old. She was undeniably a very talented and brilliant woman, and a story has grown up of her being the first computer programmer. This is a legend, but she did anticipate many features of programming. However, her association of the Jacquard loom with programming, when she said 'The Analytical Engine weaves algebraic patterns, just as the Jacquard loom weaves flowers and leaves,' was purely metaphorical. What Ada Lovelace meant was that recorded programs could induce computation machines to follow a plan of action with algebraic rigour, and not just for numerical quantities:

> The engine can arrange and combine its numerical quantities exactly as if they were letters or any other general symbols; and in fact it might bring out its results in algebraical notation, were provisions made accordingly.[3]

Despite these rather exotic origin myths, and the growing use of punched tape, ticker tape would not really become a dominant medium of message recording until the advent of Murray's printing telegraph, which combined the typewriter with Baudot's digital code and sender. Murray's combination of the typewriter with Baudot's code would lead to an almost overnight explosion of the use of ticker tape – paper tape with holes punched into it using Baudot's code for sending messages – at the beginning of the twentieth century. The iconic images we see in the movies, of financiers of the 1920s and '30s fingering paper tape emerging from a small glass-domed device, were of the printed stock prices printed onto paper tape using the Baudot–Murray code.

The mass of paper tape produced from these devices in New York would lead to the legendary ticker-tape parades. However, as iconic as ticker tape may be, we need to first look at another technology which also arose from punching holes in paper.

Punched cards

One of the areas in which data collection and processing was exploding at the end of the nineteenth century was that of the population census. By the 1880 census in the U.S., after the country had experienced a ten-fold increase in population over the previous ninety years, it took the U.S. Census Bureau a full seven and a half years to process the results. At that time, the census was recorded onto large pre-printed forms, with the data being written down into the appropriate columns. This data was then counted and recorded at numerous levels by a small army of clerks and 'computors' – people who calculated sums and statistics by hand. This was a laborious and time-consuming process, with lots of cross-checking, hence the very long time needed to process the census statistics. As the census was such an important source of information for the formulation of governmental policy, such a delay was untenable. An alternative approach was desperately needed. In search of a solution, the U.S. Census Bureau held a competition in 1888 to find a way to alleviate delay in the forthcoming 1890 census. The competition was won by a young employee of the Census Bureau, Herman Hollerith.

The system that Hollerith had developed during the 1880s was already working by the beginning of the 1890 census and was immediately applied. The reason that the new, somewhat untested system was implemented at once was that the Census Bureau had estimated that with the then current counting methods, the 1890 census would take a minimum of twelve years to finish. This meant that they would have the embarrassing situation of having two censuses running at the same time. As a result of applying Hollerith's new counting system, the 1890s census took a mere six weeks to count and the entire census was completed in two and a half years.

Hollerith was a statistician with the Census Bureau and had been working on the problem of processing large amounts of data since graduating from university in 1880. During a brief courtship with a Kate Sherman Billings, Hollerith met her father, Dr John Shaw Billings, who was the head of the Census Bureau's Department of Vital Statistics. Despite the courtship not lasting very long, Dr Billings took a liking to the young Hollerith and gave him advice and encouragement. It seems that Billings also provided Hollerith with the idea of using paper with punched holes to record the categorical information about individuals in the census.

There are two stories about how Hollerith came up with this idea. One comes from Hollerith himself when, years later, he recounted how, while travelling on a train in the early 1880s, he noticed that to prevent multiple passengers from using the same ticket, train companies would punch out characteristics of the passenger on the pre-printed ticket. If a young woman was travelling, the issuing ticket officer would punch 'female', 'young', some indication of height, hair colour and, being the nineteenth century, her skin colour as well. This was not really using a code, but simply indicating the presence of physical attributes.

This is a credible story as this is precisely the system later used by Hollerith for his punched cards. The cards were pre-printed with different census categories in sections, and individual attributes with punch locations. A hole punched at a location indicated the presence of that attribute for the individual.

However, another story has it that Hollerith got the idea from Dr Billings, who suggested to him early in their acquaintance that he should consider the system of the Jacquard loom. It is clear that Hollerith's first tabulating machine was inspired in part by the Jacquard loom, though it owed more to the player piano. The first version of his tabulating machine, patented in 1884, used a continuous paper feed. However, it used a drum to make an electrical connection through the punched hole, which was completely unlike the Jacquard loom.

Two problems immediately arose for Hollerith's system. First, the paper strip, which couldn't be as robust as the very thick Jacquard loom cards, tore easily, resulting in many hours of repair and recovering the feed. The second problem was that it was extremely difficult

1	1	3	0	2	4	10	On	S	A	C	E	a	c	e	g		EB	SB	Ch	Sy	U	Sh	Hk	Br	Rm
2	2	4	1	3	E	15	Off	IS	B	D	F	b	d	f	h		SY	X	Fp	Cn	R	X	Al	Cg	Kg
3	0	0	0	0	W	20		0	0	0	0	0	0	0	0	0	0	0	0	0	0	0	0	0	0
A	1	1	1	1	0	25	A	1	1	1	1	1	1	1	1	1	1	1	1	1	1	1	1	1
B	2	2	2	2	5	30	B	2	2	2	2	2	2	2	2	2	2	2	2	2	2	2	2	2
C	3	3	3	3	0	3	C	3	3	3	3	3	3	3	3	3	3	3	3	3	3	3	3	3
D	4	4	4	4	1	4	D	4	4	4	4	4	4	4	4	4	4	4	4	4	4	4	4	4
E	5	5	5	5	2	C	E	5	5	5	5	5	5	5	5	5	5	5	5	5	5	5	5	5
F	6	6	6	6	A	D	F	6	6	6	6	6	6	6	6	6	6	6	6	6	6	6	6	6
G	7	7	7	7	B	E	G	7	7	7	7	7	7	7	7	7	7	7	7	7	7	7	7	7
H	8	8	8	8	a	F	H	8	8	8	8	8	8	8	8	8	8	8	8	8	8	8	8	8
I	9	9	9	9	b	c	I	9	9	9	9	9	9	9	9	9	9	9	9	9	9	9	9	9

Herman Hollerith's punched card from the 1890 U.S. census.

Jacquard loom, 19th century, with the punched cards corresponding to the weaving pattern.

to find an individual record on the long paper strip. Though this first patented tabulating machine was produced, and even used, in 1885 by the U.S. Navy, Hollerith soon developed a new tabulating system, which he patented on 8 June 1887, using stiff cards the size of a U.S. dollar bill, so as to utilize existing banking storage systems. It was this design that Hollerith presented for the Census Bureau competition and which was so successful in tabulating the results of the 1890 census.

With the success of the 1887 'electric tabulating system', Hollerith went on to create a company to manufacture and market the new system based on punched cards and rapid electric circuit tabulation. The Tabulating Machine Company, founded in 1896 with Herman Hollerith at its head, grew at an immense speed as the potential of the new technology was quickly realized. Just fifteen years later, Charles Ranlett Flint, an American businessman, bought the Tabulating

Machine Company for $2.3 million, an immense amount at the time. Flint bought Hollerith's company as part of a merger of four new business technology firms to create the Computing-Tabulating-Recording Company (CTR) in 1911. Keeping Hollerith on the board of directors of CTR, Flint also appointed a convicted felon, Thomas J. Watson Sr, as managing director. Watson had been convicted of various anti-trust violations, but managed never to actually go to prison. He brought a strong, albeit villainous, brand of management to the new CTR, developing it into an international business within ten years.

Watson's most famous contribution to CTR – we will not comment on his many infamous contributions[4] – was his rebranding of the company, in 1924, as International Business Machines – IBM. The development of the punched card, from Hollerith's company to Big Blue, would have a profound effect on the application of punched cards and their relationship with digital codes. This was not a direct relationship, but was due mainly to two factors. First, IBM in the 1920s and '30s was a rapidly expanding company that pegged its success and reputation on research and development. As a result, IBM hired some really talented engineers who worked on a number of innovative technologies at this time. Second, tabulation technology had, by the 1920s and '30s, become a very competitive industry. IBM, like its primary competitor, Remington Rand, the same Remington that produced the first typewriters, needed constant innovation, in both its technologies and the services it offered, to stay competitive – much like the current IT industries.

Storing data: development of the IBM punch card

Since the First World War, punched card technology had come into ubiquitous use by governments, the military and most businesses, especially the new rail and utility companies, as well as banks and large department stores. However, these punched cards, as we discussed before, were not strings of characters, but were purpose-printed for tabulating – summing up – different categories. So a card for the census would show your gender, a hole punched if you were a man or a woman; your age, a hole if you were 20–30, 30–40 and so on; a hole for your occupation; and so on. These would be summed up by literally running the cards through a machine that counted the numbers of holes for each category, and further calculated by large machines made by the likes of IBM and Remington Rand. One of the problems with these tabulators was, however, that to both record the output of the calculations, and to transfer the results of one calculation to the next machine, the results had to be read from dials and written down by hand, or hand-punched onto a new card. This was not only time-consuming but was prone to error.

Competition between tabulating companies was intense, and IBM decided to try to gain an edge over its competitors by finding a way to increase the amount of categorical information that could be included on a punched card, and to print directly onto the card. It was the work of simply increasing the amount of categorical information that could be punched onto a card that led to the solution of the other problem of recording, storing and then rereading messages for processing.

One of IBM's leading engineers, Clair D. Lake, started working in the late 1920s on new designs to increase the amount and diversity of information that could be put on the punched cards. Lake was one of IBM's chief engineers working at their facility in Endicott, New York. In 1928, Lake developed, with his assistants George Daly and Ralph Page, what would become the ubiquitous 80-column IBM punched card. The original purpose of the new card was to provide more than double the amount of information that had been possible before on the 45-column Hollerith cards, and its impact was rapid and significant. For the first time, a card could carry sufficient information for it to be used in a vast number of diverse applications.

Though the 80-column IBM card could still be organized as a categorical table, the primary purpose of the development, initiated by IBM's president Thomas Watson, was to create a card that could encode numbers and characters as well as categorical information. The initial project was a competition between two groups at IBM working in isolation from each other. It was Clair's group who won with an 80-column card, launched in 1928, initially with ten rows of rectangular punched holes, rather than the more common round holes. The initial ten rows represented an encoding of numbers, but were expanded to twelve rows in 1930 to accommodate letter characters.

The new IBM 80-column card was an almost instant success, allowing for rapid printing and transfer of data between systems, and thus rapid accounting of all sorts of governmental and business transactions. This was because the new card, rather than being organized by the presence or absence of a category, allowed each column to be flexibly assigned to up to twelve different categories or to represent a number or letter character using digital encoding. Though not using the Baudot–Murray code, this led to both more flexible and more rapid processing of information, and the recording, storing and rereading of information. The new IBM card, for the first time, allowed the information encoded onto it to also be printed along the top of the card. This meant that not only could the card be tabulated, but it could be used to print out the results, store information and results of tabulations, and allow this information to be reread for further processing, as well as read by humans.

Remington Rand, IBM's main competitor, then came out with a 90-column card, but IBM had already come to dominate the market. The new large department stores in the U.S. would use these new punched cards to document transactions at the till (cash register), with the columns documenting the item number, time and date of the purchase as well as other important information direct from the sales desk to the accounting office. Most significantly, the new U.S. Social Security system, introduced in 1935, used the new IBM punched cards to keep track of all aspects of the system's administration from the names and addresses of the initial 53,000 recipients, to their benefits, status, payments and so on. The Second World War was largely administered – by both sides – on these 80-column punched cards.

Though the 80 columns of twelve punch points would become generic in tabulation from the 1930s, as with Hollerith's original

A data card from IBM's Selective Sequence Electronic Calculator (SSEC), built at IBM's Endicott facility by Wallace Eckert in 1946–7.

cards, categories, not digital codes, were punched into these cards. The original Social Security punched data card shows how the columns were divided into categories, and the punch points used as attributes from 2 to 12. This was not digitized information, using a digital code, but, rather, more flexible presences and absences of categorical attributes designed for the various information uses.

Originally the IBM card had ten rows, each representing a numeral from 0 to 9. In 1930, two more rows were added. When a combination of these two control rows was punched, the IBM machinery would interpret punches in the lower ten rows as character codes. However, the codes used on cards were different from those used in the telegraph industry, the Baudot–Murray code. This was initially because there was no good reason to utilize the Baudot–Murray code, as the IBM codes were only to be used on IBM tabulating machinery and needed to be optimized for calculations and sorting.

By the mid-1930s many office machine companies had printers, readers and accounting machines that used digital character encoding on cards, but, unlike the telecommunications industry, which had just standardized its encoding, more or less every tabulation manufacturer had its own encoding. For many, these encodings were flexible and could be altered depending on the machine and its uses, as the industry, and its customers, had little interest in their information being

Social Security office, Baltimore, Maryland, in 1937. All these clerks are punching and sorting punched cards.

used across systems. Unlike in the telecommunications industry, the principle in tabulation systems was that as each machine had its own particular function, or set of functions, and as there was only transfer of media from one machine to another in particular instances, and never from one manufacturer to another, there was no need for standardized encoding. This situation continued up to the 1960s, as, even with the early electronic digital computers, speaking to the computer via character codes and its printing back to you were always limited to a single platform from a single manufacturer. There was no need for standardization across the industry, even across a range of machines from a single vendor. It is not until the 1960s, when there was a growing need for information sharing between machines – machines often from different vendors – that we find the rise of standardized character encoding for computational devices. Primarily, though, the later standardization of character codes resulted from the development of programming languages. When computers began to be controlled by a set of commands that were written with characters and numbers, as we do today, there came to be a need for standardized character codes.

There was no such delay within telecommunications, though. For the transmission of telegrams and telex, the principle of what today we would call interoperability remained as strong as ever. In the transmission of messages via telegraph or via telex, we see that throughout the first half of the twentieth century the Baudot–Murray code dominated. As we saw above, there were variations of even this code, mostly for military use, but the Baudot–Murray code remained astonishingly stable until the 1960s.

IBM's BCD code

In a patent application submitted by IBM engineer A. W. Mills in 1932, there was mention of a 'novel zoning mechanism', which described a means of encoding numerals and letters onto IBM's new 80-column card using the bottom ten rows in conjunction with the upper rows 11 and 12. What became known as the BCD, or binary-coded decimal, code had been developed for IBM's tabulating machines. BCD used the twelve-row IBM card where the bottom ten rows represented the numerals 0–9 if only one of the bottom ten rows was punched with a hole – the first row punched would be the number 0, the second row 1, third row 2, and so forth. However, if the eleventh or twelfth row was also punched then it would represent a letter. For example, if the twelfth and the first row were punched, then it would be the capital letter 'A', the twelfth and the second row would be a 'B', and so forth. There was no need to reorder the letters to gain efficiency, as the combinations would use the same number of punches, two, for each character, except for a few of the special characters which had three holes.

The BCD code was extremely popular and persistent. Not only was it the primary punched card code for IBM until the 1960s, but Burroughs, Bull, CDC, General Electric, NCR, Siemens and Sperry Univac all also adopted the BCD code for their early electronic computers from the

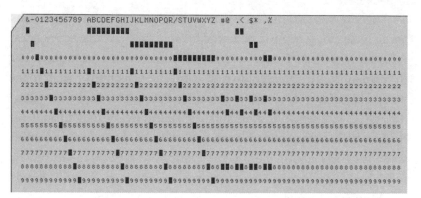

IBM (026) card showing the punched codes for all the character codes.

late 1940s. However, BCD would not survive the digital computing expansion of the late 1950s and early 1960s.

EBCDIC

Though the development and use of BCD was a bit of a sideshow in the development of digital codes, its successor was not. The Extended Binary-Coded Decimal Interchange Code (EBCDIC) was the first IBM-designed encoding for use with digital computers. In fact, due to the success of IBM's early digital mainframe computer, the IBM 360, EBCDIC almost became a predominant standard for encoding characters.

EBCDIC was developed, in 1963 and 1964, so that IBM could not only encode lower-case letters, but could add control characters necessary for processing the data on electronic computers. At this time, IBM was playing a double game. It was one of the chief corporate proponents of a new standard, ASCII (more of this later), but it continued to develop its own in-house character encoding. This was largely because so many of its legacy peripherals, such as printers, duplicating punches and card punches, were built for BCD. Computing hardware, in the 1960s, remained almost as diverse as the tabulating hardware of the 1930s and '40s.

EBCDIC was rolled out with IBM's new general-purpose, programmable mainframe computer, the IBM 360. Though the 360 had some 'tolerance' for ASCII encoded files, IBM could not change all its peripherals in time for the 360 launch, so they kept EBCDIC. In practice, this didn't seem to be much of a problem, as peripherals were quickly developed to translate cards from EBCDIC to ASCII and back. However, EBCDIC lacked a number of important punctuation codes, such as curly brackets, that were used in the new programming languages. EBCDIC also sorted characters with lower-case letters first, while ASCII sorted with upper-case first.

Despite these differences and incompatibilities, and largely due to IBM's dominance at the time, a number of encodings remained in use until the early 1980s. By the end of the 1960s, IBM and many other computer companies were using EBCDIC or proprietary encodings – though even IBM used no fewer than nine encodings on its various devices. The military continued to use FIELDATA, though it was increasingly promoting ASCII. At this time, only UNIVAC was using ASCII, and it was only exclusively used on its UNIVAC 1050, an offline peripheral controller. The only other exception to this almost universal ostracizing of ASCII was in telecommunications.

Standardized character codes

ASCII

From the end of the 1950s there was an enormous growth in computing machinery and its scope. The first programming codes were being developed (FORTRAN and COBAL), and the control of computer systems by 'languages', literally through the use of systematic words and phrases, was developing fast. Not only this, but the shift from computers as specific-purpose computational devices to general, programmable, information processing systems was well under way. This meant that there was an urgent need for a standardized means of encoding the vast amount of text, using a wide range of characters, that was being entered into, and processed by, computers; text that now was the primary means of not only representing information, but of controlling the computer itself and its processes.

In 1960 the American Standards Association (ASA) created the x3.2 subcommittee whose purpose was to develop a standard digital code for upper- and lower-case Latin letters, the numerals and various punctuation and control characters. It was not to be an extension of the many industry codes, but was to be an extension of the existing telegraphic codes, the Baudot–Murray codes. The first meeting of the x3.2 subcommittee was held on 6 October 1960, but the final standard was not published until 1963.

The x3.2 subcommittee had to accommodate the encoding needs of the ITA2 standard of what was now, since 1956, the Comité Consultatif International Téléphonique et Télégraphique (CCITT), FIELDATA and the EBCDIC of IBM. This meant that they would have to accommodate more than the 64 characters of the Baudot–Murray code (ITA2), so a 5-bit, or even a 6-bit, code would not suffice. So it was clear from the start that ASCII (American Standard Code for Information Interchange) would be a 7-bit code. Largely following FIELDATA, ASCII would focus, though, on the order of the characters in the digital sequence. What this means is that the developers of ASCII were keenly aware that this code would not just be used for telegraph and telex messages, but also for processing information. So there were two key features of ASCII that distinguished it from earlier character codes. First, all the control characters were placed at the front of the sequence to make it easier for both telegraph systems and information systems to process them. Second, ASCII was explicitly designed to make it easier to order data alphabetically and numerically by sorting the digital codes themselves. ASCII was a character code specifically designed for the new digital information processing systems, what we call computers.

What distinguished ASCII most was its extraordinary success. Going through several revisions from 1967 to the final version in 1986, almost from the beginning ASCII was the dominant character encoding for all digital character data. Into the 1970s and '80s, only a few special-purpose systems, mainly military systems, used older or other encodings. With the rise of the minicomputer in the 1970s and the microcomputer at the beginning of the 1980s, ASCII was virtually the only character encoding to be found. This was also true for telecommunications systems. The first use of ASCII was for Bell Corporation's (AT&T) teleprinter systems. For all digital encoding, whether in telecommunications or in computer processing, ASCII was the encoding for characters, numbers and punctuation. It was the encoding that the entire computing industry, the one we know today with our laptops, mobile phones and smart devices, grew up on.

010 0000	(space)	011 1000	8	101 0000	P	110 1000	h
010 0001	!	011 1001	9	101 0001	Q	110 1001	i
010 0010	o	011 1010	:	101 0010	R	110 1010	j
010 0011	#	011 1011	;	101 0011	S	110 1011	k
010 0100	$	011 1100	<	101 0100	T	110 1100	l
010 0101	%	011 1101	=	101 0101	U	110 1101	m
010 0110	&	011 1110	>	101 0110	V	110 1110	n
010 0111	'	011 1111	?	101 0111	W	110 1111	o
010 1000	(	100 0000	@	101 1000	X	111 0000	p
010 1001	)	100 0001	A	101 1001	Y	111 0001	q
010 1010	*	100 0010	B	101 1010	Z	111 0010	r
010 1011	+	100 0011	C	101 1011	[	111 0011	s
010 1100	,	100 0100	D	101 1100	\	111 0100	t
010 1101	-	100 0101	E	101 1101	]	111 0101	u
010 1110	.	100 0110	F	101 1110	^	111 0110	v
010 1111	/	100 0111	G	101 1111	_	111 0111	w
011 0000	0	100 1000	H	110 0000	`	111 1000	x
011 0001	1	100 1001	I	110 0001	a	111 1001	y
011 0010	2	100 1010	J	110 0010	b	111 1010	z
011 0011	3	100 1011	K	110 0011	c	111 1011	{
011 0100	4	100 1100	L	110 0100	d	111 1100	|
011 0101	5	100 1101	M	110 0101	e	111 1101	}
011 0110	6	100 1110	N	110 0110	f	111 1110	~
011 0111	7	100 1111	O	110 0111	g		

ASCII 8-bit code developed from the Baudot–Murray code and the ITA2.

It was not until the end of the 1980s, with the proliferation of microcomputers to all parts of the world, and all communities, and into all languages, that a new encoding was needed; an encoding that could handle the literally thousands of characters from hundreds of languages, and a limitless variety of graphic symbols. When digital devices found themselves having to work not just in English and a few European languages, but in Hindi, Chinese, Japanese, even Cherokee and Inuit, the number of characters exploded. What emerged was what we have today: an efficient and unpretentious encoding that owes much of its foundation to ASCII and, hence, even to Murray and Baudot – Unicode.

Unicode

Though we still live in a world of many different character encodings, Unicode is the character encoding that most of our devices use today. If you are writing on your iPad or iPhone, or on an Android device, typing into a laptop or a desktop, texting on your smartwatch or even entering code on a supercomputer, chances are you are using Unicode. Unicode was developed for a very particular, and today very familiar, market – personal computing. In 1987 an engineer from Xerox named Joe Becker, and two engineers, Lee Collins and Mark Davis, from a very young company, Apple, decided to work on a truly universal character set.[5] For both Becker at Xerox and Collins and Davis at Apple, the encoding problem at the end of the 1980s was how to accommodate an enormous character set, literally how to encode all of the character scripts, symbols and numerals in the world. This would not only need a much longer bit code for each character, but a completely different approach.

Originally Becker assumed that the new code would only have to accommodate existing characters of the world's living languages, in other words those that were in print in 1989. This was not a huge undertaking in 1989, but even then required a vastly extended encoding. So though Unicode was an extension of ASCII, with the first 256 code points made identical to the content of ASCII, Unicode adopted a 16-bit encoding to provide a vast number of possibilities. The first version (1991) included over 7,000 characters including Arabic, Hebrew, diverse Indian scripts and even Tibetan. With the 16-bit encoding, version 1.1 (1993) had encoded over 34,000 characters.

Another unique aspect of Unicode was that it was developed with personal computers in mind, and specifically the new Apple computers which allowed for WYSIWYG ('what you see is what you get') word processors. Unlike earlier character encodings, Unicode did not directly encode the character, but created a number, a reference, that the computer could use to process the letter, adding features to it such as font, size, italics, bold and so on. The computers we use today are clearly accepted as media machines, not simply character or information processors, but this requires bundling the character encoding with information about its presentation, how it would look on the screen, so that the identity of the letter and how it would look were both resolved by processing. Up until the 1980s, except for a few research applications, the dominant method of entering text had not changed much since Murray's time. You punched a keyboard, which stored encoded letters, and the encoded letters were printed by getting a mechanical type to punch an inked tape onto paper. Unicode set what is now the standard form of working with text on digital devices, where only the keyboard remains – all the rest is processed, including the printer. Where Murray detached the encoding from the letter, Unicode would remove any representational role of the encoding, leaving this to decisions of a process, or an application, to decide. From then on, characters were merely processed images, connected merely by conventions imposed by programs. Digitality had become nothing but code.

By June 1992, Unicode had encoded all the existing printable character sets found in the world at that time. However, even this enormous expansion to a 16-bit code could not encompass the needs of the World Wide Web, which would burst onto the world only one year later. By the end of the 1990s, there was a need for so many character sets that even Unicode had to be extended. What we use today are various versions of the 1996 Unicode 2.0, which is a surrogate character system no longer limited to 16 bits. By designating a surrogate system, one that allows you to designate a number of properties for each code point and to designate various code sets in the encoding, Unicode today has the possibility of encoding over one million different characters. As of 2015, with Unicode 8.0, a variant of Unicode 2.0, we now have access to almost 121,000 characters, so there is still plenty of room for more.

With Unicode, the fonts we now use, the letters and numerals we now type and print, are, like all the other objects on our digital devices, mediated. We no longer have simple encoded letters, any more than we have simple encoded images. All these digital objects are complex processes that result in diverse renderings of the key we once pressed. But we have some more ground to cover before we can fully expand on this accomplishment.

In the early 1970s, it seemed that the development of computers had reached its apogee and could not go much further. The situation for encoding seemed as though it would remain as it was, with a diversity of large computing platforms, each doing rather well-defined jobs, using a diversity of encodings that were somewhat different from those used for telecommunications. However, this was to change with the rise of the personal computer. Though we will talk about the rise of the PC in Chapter Five, the 1970s heralded a new age in computing, and, again, a decision by IBM would transform the fortune of character encoding.

If I can get a bit ahead of myself with a brief aside, the fate of character encoding was laid to rest by a surprise decision by IBM in 1980. IBM brought out its personal computer rather late, in 1981. Some companies had been manufacturing and selling personal computers for several years by then. Hewlett-Packard had marketed its 9100A as early as 1968, with Atari, Commodore and even Apple offering personal computers by the end of the 1970s. However, being dominant in the mainframe and minicomputer fields, IBM had the capacity to dominate the personal computer market. When they released their first IBM personal computer, to the surprise of almost everyone, it was based on ASCII. As IBM would run Microsoft's first MS-DOS, a combination that would dominate personal computing for over twenty years, and because of the fact that Apple was already dedicated to ASCII, it seemed that the future of miscellaneous character encodings was over. From then on, except for some very specialist applications, ASCII and then Unicode would dominate as the Baudot–Murray code had come to dominate telecommunications.

Aside from the obvious advantages of duplication and storage, the ability of digital codes to allow the almost endless copying and printing of messages onto various storage media created another advance in communications technology: the ability to transmit messages from one type of mechanism to a completely different one. Before common digital codes, the only way to calibrate message transmission and reception was either to use experienced coders, as with the Morse system, or to use identical, calibrated mechanisms at both ends, as with the Hughes system. Today, this would be similar to being able to email your colleague only after you and they went through series of calibrations between your two devices, monitoring the sending of the message and recalibrating your devices afterwards. This would also only be possible if you both had the same make, and often the same model, of laptop or mobile. However, the use of a common digital code that transmitted to a printing medium, or any storage medium, allowed for the use of heterogeneous mechanisms at all points on the storage, transmission and processing chain. As long as all the devices and mechanisms accepted the same code, they could all work in unison even though they had no technology or mechanisms in common. Today, we do not worry what device our colleague or friend has when we send them an SMS or email or share something on Twitter. A shared, and accepted, code is all that is needed. We can, if we wish, process the code differently, accommodating our desires and local preferences. Today, our many digital devices work in concert because the digital objects we access are digital, having a common, shared encoding.

None of these developments was simple or self-evident. They were, and remain, complex achievements. What these developments in common encoding within heterogeneous networks, and local processing, have enabled, though, is an explosion in telecommunications and information processing. This chapter in the history of telecommunications, now largely forgotten, began with the development of a digital means of long-distance communication which would dominate telecommunications from the 1920s to the 1970s. However, this history did not finish with the end of digital telecommunications, but continued with the procession of digital codes that arose to fill the growing needs of the industry – personal computing. The history of codes would lead directly to the digital character encoding that, in the 1960s, would be appropriated for the new needs of computing to store, transmit and process its growing quantity of digitally encoded information: digital codes whose successors are allowing me to type this text now.

3
REVISITING COMPUTATION: COMPUTATION DOESN'T NEED TO BE DIGITAL

The necessity of computation: computers and analogues

On 10 April 1872, while Baudot was still working on his first prototypes, the 4th Ordinary General Meeting of the Society of Telegraph Engineers was being held in London. The subject of their discussion was neither digital nor Morse telegraph codes, as these engineers were not interested in the content of telegraph transmissions. They were concerned with a more practical problem: electricity.

Obviously, telegraph systems run on electrical currents, and we often think of this as a completely trivial problem. However, as today, telecommunications networks must be built and maintained and, most of all, must work. This requires a great deal of engineering. In the mid-nineteenth century, with the rise of the telegraph, there also arose a new discipline, electrical engineering. It was the job of the new electrical engineers to determine not only how the wires should be run, but how they should, and even could, be powered.

This was an enormously complicated job, as it is today. The problem was, at first sight, a relatively straightforward one. Telegraph lines from station to station had to have sufficient power, boosted at intervals along the way, to ensure that a readable signal could be transmitted and received. However, with the new telegraph systems, engineers were not dealing with simple lines, but with vast, interconnected and complex *networks*. The investment was enormous, and mistakes would always be costly. The role of this new breed of engineers, electrical engineers, was to determine not only how much power was needed at each segment of the network, but how this power would interact across the network. A surge at one point in the network would impact transmissions, even the viability, of other segments. Power outages in one place could bring down whole sections of the network, if not properly designed for.

The modelling of these interactions involved a great deal of mathematics and number crunching. The infrastructure that would process the vast mathematics and equations needed to model even a small part of the network had, by the 1870s, become a major investment by the telegraph companies. This infrastructure employed two developments that were new to the nineteenth century: one was an occupation, the other a technology. The technology and the occupation were entangled as the purpose of both was to solve mathematical equations – to *compute*.

Increasingly, by the mid-nineteenth century, the computors were assisted in their computations by a growing technology – calculators. It was both the calculators themselves and their applications which the chairman of the 1872 meetings in London described as matters 'of great interest'.[1] The debate was about the Arithmometer, an early calculating machine, and its use in electrical calculations. The argument was interesting in that it did not centre around how to use the calculator, the Arithmometer, to assist their computors (the people doing the calculations) – this was accepted – but on the value of a mechanical calculator to ensure accuracy and efficiency. As General Hannyngton, a military man and actuary, at this point retired and holding the position of assistant secretary of the Finance Department of the India Office, saw it, the value of the Arithmometer was that it did not tire:

> even where calculations were not of an arduous nature, or such as to occasion any great strain upon the mind, after some hours' work the head would get weary, whereas this machine always remained perfect cool.[2]

The Arithmometer was a mechanical calculator, it was operated by dials, levers and cranks, without any electricity, and it was built upon earlier models of mechanical calculators from the eighteenth century. More and more quickly, though, in the late nineteenth century, calculation and computation were becoming electrical.

By the end of the nineteenth century, computation was everywhere. Not only were the telegraph and telephone networks growing rapidly, but other networks were expanding. Railways, electrical power transmissions, economic and commercial networks all were becoming increasingly complex and interconnected, requiring vast amounts of calculation. Technological networks were increasingly calculated and computed, and the rising national censuses and insurance industries required vast statistical and actuarial computations. The new field of statistics created a need in business and government for greater statistical measures of everything from characterizations of the population, to population movements and demographics, to economic changes, to racial characterizations.[3] Not only were the engineering problems computed, but all aspects of business, government and people were increasingly computed – reckoned and rendered with numbers. All this was achieved by a vast number of computers (or computors).

However, we must remember that these computors were people, not machines. It is estimated that, in the 1870s, the country that had the most computors was India – a situation that may be repeated in the not too distant future. When the 4th Ordinary General Meeting of the Society of Telegraph Engineers was considering the Arithmometer in London in 1872, the superintendent of the Grand Trigonometrical Survey of India, Colonel Walker, commented that he thought the Arithmometer could be useful for computation in India, despite the fact that there were so many skilful 'native' computors, who were available at a very low price.[4]

By the beginning of the twentieth century, however, there was a real crisis in computation. Though the human computor had developed into a full-blown industry and profession, yielding very accurate and precise results, it remained very slow. Teams of computors would work on a specific calculation over many months, checking and rechecking their results. Even with mechanical calculators, the task was laborious, tedious and error-prone.

Recalling the calculations for the electrification of the Virginian Railroad in the 1920s, H. A. Travers, an electrical engineer at Westinghouse, characterized the process:

> two crews of three men each worked several months with a battery of adding machines making the necessary calculations of short-circuit currents, voltage regulation, and telephone interference for the almost endless combinations of circuits and loads. Each team would work furiously for a couple of weeks, and then spend the next week or so checking the results of the other team. With other railroad electrifications in the offing, with power systems growing so large and so complex in their interconnection, the solution of power-system problems by mathematics was becoming a monumental task and in many cases utterly hopeless.[5]

Analogue computation: calculating by analogy

The Arithmometer that was discussed at the 1872 meeting of the telegraph engineers was a mechanical calculator. Such calculators had been designed, and a few even built, in the eighteenth century, though the Arithmometer was the first to go into large-scale production. The principle was simple, though the mechanisms could be very complex and the accuracies were critical. The principle was that by combining a series of gears, cogs, rods and pulleys in a synchronized structure, these connected mechanisms could be turned, by hand, so as to model systematically the actions of calculating, adding and subtracting numbers, by analogy with the movement of these gears, rods and pulleys. What this means is that by placing ten equidistant teeth on a gear, the proportion of each tooth of the gear is analogous to one of the ten decimal numbers (0–9). What these devices did was to model numbers as an analogy of distance. By aligning a number of gears, each with ten equidistant teeth, you could make your device combine numbers and calculate them by simply moving the synchronized gears through a specified distance.

Another form of computation by analogy that was being used from the middle of the nineteenth century was to actually model, in miniature, the electrical network that you needed to measure. These electrical analysers were literally a scale model of the network that was being examined. On a large table – and they were often called 'artificial electric lines' or 'short-circuit calculating tables' – engineers would assemble a number of electrical components which would act in a sufficiently analogous way to the electrical lines, boosters, loads and connections that they were proposing to build. This analogue electrical network could then be powered, and changes in loads along different lines and at specific points and connections could be tried out and the impact on all the network measured directly.

These network analysers were basically scaled-down models of the electrical properties of an electrical power grid. However, rather than actually build a model of the electrical network – though this was sometimes done – generators, lines and loads were replaced with small electrical components whose input and output were proportional to the system being modelled. Some of these network analysers were fixed analogues of actual systems, while others were more flexible mechanisms which could be configured using power cords plugged into plugboards like an old-style telephone exchange. Since the electrical analysers were mostly a series of power sources connected to a network of capacitances, resistances and inductances – basically the electronic bits you need to increase or decrease electrical current – these analysers could be, and were, used to model just about any 'network' problem: electrical loads and resistances, even 'outages', also seen as analogous to flows of natural resources, the movement of goods in the economy, population movements, or interactions of capital. As today, such socio-economic problems were modelled using algorithms and mathematical models. The electrical analyser was a computer that allowed such models to be built and run, using different parameters, or criteria. However, rather than using digital logic to run a program to emulate the model, these computers ran the model by physical, or electrical, analogy. But more of this in a bit.

As networks, and their models, grew in extent and complexity, the network analysers grew in complexity as well. In 1919, a young scientist, Vannevar Bush, had just joined the teaching staff of the Department of Electrical Engineering at MIT (Massachusetts Institute of Technology), in Cambridge, Massachusetts. Three years earlier he had completed, in one year, his doctorate at MIT on 'Oscillating-current Circuits: An Extension of the Theory of Generalized Angular Velocities, with Applications to the Coupled Circuit and the Artificial Transmission Line'. In his dissertation, finished far too quickly according to his supervisor, he had proposed a new modelling concept for power systems that used a transformer (a device for increasing or reducing electrical current) to represent the loads within the network analyser. In principle, this allowed for much greater accuracy and complexity in the analysis, and his model was put to the test at the end of the 1920s. In a joint project between MIT and General Electric, a network analyser (the MIT Network Analyzer) was first demonstrated in June 1929. It consisted of eight phase-shifting transformers, using Bush's design, to represent synchronous machines, 100 variable reactors, 100 variable line resistors, 32 fixed capacitors, and 40 adjustable load units. A very large electrical device, it was spread over four panels arranged in a U, with tables in front for the sensitive thermocouple instruments for measuring the interactions.[6] Though primarily a proof-of-concept analyser, and for teaching purposes, the MIT Network Analyzer saw considerable use by outside companies throughout the 1930s and '40s.

Though these network analysers were used to model all sorts of network problems well into the 1950s, they were increasingly being made redundant by other, more flexible and accurate, technologies. Not, however, yet, digital technologies. In fact, what is most interesting about this period of innovation in computation and modelling is that none of it even anticipated digital computers or utilized existing digital technologies.[7] That was yet to come.

What is analogue computing?

The idea of calculating by making a machine that models calculations by analogy is very old indeed. One of the earliest timepieces, or clocks, is the hourglass. The hourglass may have been in use over 2,000 years ago, and is a good example of an analogue computer. The sand falling through a small hole in the glass vessel, controlling in a regulated way the amount of sand passing through, models by analogy the passing of time. This means that the hourglass can 'measure' time as a function of sand accumulating in the bottom of the glass.

History is full of analogue computers, some, but not all, associated with *computing* time. We find not only hourglasses, but sundials and water clocks, all of which modelled time by the change in volume of some material or position of some regular relationship (for example, of the earth to the sun). Even mechanical clocks are analogue devices, as they model time as a function of distance around gears, pulleys or cogs. However, analogue computers were also found wherever there was a need to calculate, model or measure. As we discussed above, there were mechanical calculators in the eighteenth century – calculators based on an analogue of calculation as movement through space. There were also electrical analysers and other network modellers. We find many devices for drafting, planning and mapping being used. Sextants, used by mariners to determine their latitude at sea, are an analogue computer, as are the much older astrolabes for calculating astronomical movements. More up to date, almost all recording and broadcast media of the nineteenth and twentieth centuries were analogue devices. Film gave the appearance of movement by passing calibrated still images through a projection device; phonographs recreate sounds by analogously engraving sound waves onto a disc; even TV and radio, until they went digital at the turn of the twenty-first century, modulated analogue radio waves modelling sound and vision. Until we all had LED screens, even our digital computers had to modulate our screens using an analogue signal.

Solving problems, in particular technical problems, by analogy was so widespread by the early twentieth century that many considered that such analogical means were synonymous with technology itself. This is not surprising as, until the electronic age of the 1950s and '60s, technology was mechanical. Even electrical devices were based on mechanical components. The idea that time, action, quantities, economic interaction, transmission, population growth and even social problems could be modelled by analogy with mechanical distances, surface shapes or volumes seemed an obvious one. So it is not surprising that this presupposition for analogy extended even into mathematics and calculation.

Since the seventeenth century, it has been known that many systems in the world can be modelled by certain forms of mathematical equations called differential equations. First introduced into mathematics by the work of Isaac Newton and Gottfried Wilhelm Leibniz, the details of what differential equations are need not bother us here, you will be happy to know. It is sufficient to know that a differential equation is any mathematical equation that states how a rate of change (a 'differential') in one variable is related to other variables. For many of us, this may remain rather opaque, but such equations are very useful for modelling how different systems operate as their inputs (variables) change and systematically cause changes in effects (differentials). Differential equations are used for a vast number of engineering problems, are pervasive in all branches of physics, biology and chemistry, and are used extensively in economic modelling. They are particularly useful in problems of classical mechanics (the movement of physical bodies in space) so have been used for centuries to predict how projectiles will move. One of the major uses of our computors, the people who calculated, was to solve differential equations to know the tracks of cannon shells – knowing, if you fired this shell with this much force in this direction with this angle with this wind speed and direction and this temperature and relative humidity, where it would land. Later, differential equations would be used to calculate how a bomb would fall from a plane and then land on its target. Such equations built into analogue calculators for computing artillery firing were pervasive in both the First and Second World Wars and were the basis of the famous Norden bombsight used by Allied bombers.

Vannevar Bush and the MIT Differential Analyzer

Differential equations were essential not only for blowing things up, but for many problems in engineering and the sciences. Thus the development of an effective computer (analogue mechanical device) for the calculation of differential equations had been an important project for many years, and was becoming a critical project by the 1920s.

The First World War had demonstrated the importance of accurate calculation of differential equations for artillery and aerial bombing, but, more so, the importance of differential equation calculation was realized in the development and extension of infrastructure at home. The enormous growth in electrical, transport and communications networks made the calculation of differential equations even more important, as had the now booming aeronautics industry. Hence, through the 1920s and '30s, many universities around the world were working on developing an effective 'differential analyser'. One of the universities that took up the challenge early on was MIT, and it was Vannevar Bush who by then was the professor in charge.

From 1927, working with his graduate students Herbert Stewart and Harold Hazen, Bush was developing what would become the MIT Differential Analyzer. This was an analogue computer that could solve differential equations with as many as eighteen independent variables. Bush later said in his autobiography, *Pieces of the Action*:

> I was trying to solve some of the problems of electric circuitry such as the ones connected with failures and blackouts in power networks, and I was thoroughly stuck because I could not solve the tough equations.[8]

Stewart had already been working with Bush to develop the Integraph, an analogue device for solving first-order differential equations.

However, it was Hazen who suggested that they try to extend the Integraph to handle second-order differential equations. The possibilities were immediately apparent to Bush, as second-order differential equations were common in the physical sciences and engineering, but difficult to solve.

From 1927 to 1931 Hazen worked on the device, producing in the end a unique design which, for the first time, incorporated both mechanical and electrical components. The room-sized Analyzer incorporated six 'Thompson' integrators, each with an electric motor. There were many metal shafts connecting the integrators and coupling their rotations, which were analogically proportional to the variables for whatever problem was being solved. There was also an 'output table' which plotted the results. The Differential Analyzer had to be 'programmed' for a specific problem by entering the data into three 'input tables' and repositioning all the shafts and gears. This job of 'programming' often took two or more days. However, with an accuracy averaging about 98 per cent, this was one of the fastest and most accurate network analysers available at the time, and was immediately put to use.

The primary use of the MIT Differential Analyzer, like the Arithmometer, was for electrical network analysis. One of the first engineers to use the Differential Analyzer was Professor Edith Clark, the first woman electrical engineer and a professor at the University of Texas at Austin. Her advanced work for General Electric Corporation on AC circuit analysis of AC power systems made good use of the new Analyzer.

Initially, though, Vannevar Bush thought of the Analyzer as merely a 'continuous integraph', as he wrote at the beginning of 1931. However, he quickly realized that the device was much more than this and actually was a general-purpose analogue computer. In another article, later in 1931, Bush labelled the device a 'differential analyzer'.[9] Bush suggests that this change of distinction was in part due to his and Hazen's realization, expressed in his second article, that their device was similar in principle to one built twenty years earlier by

Vannevar Bush working on his Differential Analyzer at MIT in 1931.

Lord Kelvin in England, for naval gunnery. Though Bush and Hazen's analyser used the same basic idea of interconnection of the integrating units as Kelvin's, they also pointed out that there was 'little resemblance to the earlier model' in detail. Bush would later remark in his autobiography that he was 'unaware of Kelvin's work until after the first differential analyzer was operational' in 1931.

Having accepted the prestigious directorship of the Carnegie Institution for Science in Washington, DC, in 1938, Bush would go on to build an even more complicated Analyzer with funding from the Rockefeller Foundation. The RDA (Rockefeller Differential Analyzer) was revolutionary, and later was to be considered one of the most important calculating machines of the Second World War.

As the mechanical analysers had to be set up by hand, usually with spanners (wrenches) over many hours and days, they were laborious to program. In addition, any wear to parts, gears or integrators could add unacceptable errors to the system. Bush overcame many of these problems with the RDA by replacing many of the mechanical devices with electronic components. Vacuum tubes, relays, sensors and amplifiers were all now controlled by a program punched onto a paper tape. This vastly reduced the error and increased the accuracy and speed of the RDA by a factor of ten over earlier differential analysers. For this reason, the RDA, and its successor the RDA2, continued in service throughout the war and well into the 1950s. One of the most famous uses of the RDA2 was for calculating, in reverse, the trajectories of the German V2 rockets at the end of the war. This allowed the Allies to discover and ultimately destroy the launching sites of these first ballistic missiles.

The RDA was a secret project whose existence was only revealed at the end of the war. However the immediate success of the MIT Differential Analyzer spawned many other projects. Douglas Hartree of Manchester University created an innovative differential analyser with his student Arthur Porter in 1934. The Manchester Differential Analyser was unique in that many of the components used parts from Meccano, a British constructor set for young children. As many a British child could tell you, Meccano was an enormously fun and versatile metal engineering set with literally thousands of different parts. This versatility was not lost on Hartree, nor were the cost savings – the Manchester device came at about one-tenth of the cost of other differential analysers.

Dozens of differential analysers, more or less on the Bush/Hazen model, were built in the 1930s and '40s. Successful differential analysers were built at the Ballistic Research Laboratory in Maryland, USA, as well as at the Moore School of Electrical Engineering at the University of Pennsylvania. In 1947, the University of California at Los Angeles (UCLA) also had a differential analyser built for them by General Electric. In Britain, besides the Meccano version at Manchester, Cambridge University, Queen's University Belfast and the Royal Aircraft Establishment in Farnborough all had analysers. Others were built in Oslo, Norway, and at the Osaka Imperial University, Japan.

Vannevar Bush was fast becoming one of the most important scientists in the U.S. The same year he was appointed president of the Carnegie Institution for Science, 1938, he was appointed director of the National Advisory Committee for Aeronautics (NACA), the predecessor of NASA, when its chairman Joseph Sweetman Ames fell ill. With the outbreak of war in Europe, and the German occupation of France, a movement arose amongst the American scientific community and the military to create an agency to coordinate scientific research and defence. A proposal from Bush and the NACA for a National Defense Research Committee (NDRA) was placed before Congress early in 1940. However, with mounting delays in Congress, Bush managed to get a meeting directly with the U.S. president, Franklin Delano Roosevelt, on 12 June 1940. It is said that by the end of the fifteen-minute meeting with the president, not only was the NDRA approved, but Bush was its director. One of Bush's first acts as director of the NDRA was to approve funding for a project proposed by Norbert Wiener, a professor of mathematics at MIT, for the construction of a computer that would become ENIAC; but we are getting ahead of ourselves.

Almost exactly a year after Bush's meeting with Roosevelt, Roosevelt established the Office of Scientific Research and Development (OSRD), again with Bush as its director. The OSRD approved and coordinated all wartime scientific research in the U.S. This meant that Bush was primarily responsible for the development of mass-produced penicillin, the development of radar, all innovations in avionics and analogue computing devices that arose from war work such as the Norden bombsight, the proximity fuse, gun directors and gun data computers but also the somewhat unsuccessful U.S. research into guided missiles and the Manhattan Project, which developed the first atomic bomb. Bush would also be a central influence, after the war, in the creation of the National Science Foundation (NSF), which remains today the primary scientific funding agency in the U.S.

Analogue before the 1950s: computational necessity

Throughout the 1940s, during and immediately after the Second World War, there was a profusion of activity, research and construction of mechanical and electronic devices for computation and information processing. The Second World War was, as all wars are, a war of information and calculation. We think of only the past twenty years as the time of hi-tech warfare, with satellites, 'smart' weapons, 'surgical' strikes and drones. However, it was the Second World War that ushered in today's hi-tech mediation of information, communications and computation, as well as automatically controlled weapons. Information, on all sides, was increasingly managed by punched card data, tabulated on electromechanical tabulators, sorters and integrators provided by the relatively new hi-tech companies such as IBM and Remington Rand. Analogue computers, rangefinders, firing calculators, bombsights, radar analysers and so on had become pervasive by the end of the war, while the never-ending battle for secrecy and codes led to an explosion of electromechanical and electronic computers.

However, aside from the Colossus, one of the first special-purpose digital computers, the information technologies coming out of the Second World War were all mechanical or electromechanical analogue devices. The only exceptions were the, by then very old, telecommunications technologies of telegraph and telex. In fact, what is most surprising about the information technologies of the late 1940s is that none of them anticipated digital computing. There were, and had been, digital computers – of sorts – and almost all telecommunications (telegraph and telex) used Baudot–Murray digital encoding, but there was little that anticipated the upcoming digital information revolution.

After his seminal and prodigious activities as director of the OSRD during the war, Vannevar Bush published a largely ignored, at the time, paper in The Atlantic Monthly.[10] Published at the close of the war, 'As We May Think' was an ambitious call for a new technology of memory. In his short article, Bush made the case for, and even offered a basic design for, a memory machine, a memory-index or memex. Many others have written about how Bush's associative trails influenced the development of the World Wide Web and hypertext,[11] and though we could spend some time here arguing why this was not completely so, or at least not simply so, this is not of central importance to our concerns here. Rather, what interests us is what memex was meant to represent, coming as it did immediately after the war, from one of the leading information scientists in the world, Vannevar Bush. It was, and was meant to be, a key landmark, even a manifesto, for changing attitudes to mechanization and what constituted information and information media.

Memex was never built, but Bush proposed a device that, using a specially constructed desk consisting of electromechanical controls, as well as microfilm cameras and readers, could become 'a sort of mechanized private file and library'.[12] What is interesting about memex is how it was conceived completely as an analogue device. Bush argued extensively in his paper for the sense of such a system in a world of exploding information. Though he referenced an extensive history of computing, from Leibniz to Babbage, he did not mention the digital or binary once. At the end of the war, for Bush and others, computation and information processing was purely an analogue problem.

Even the famous Colossus computer, which was digital, was seen as a special-purpose device, as were almost all the analogue devices of that period, whose utility did not go beyond its designed purpose of

Numeral	Baudot's 5-bit code*	ascii 8-bit code	Binary number
0	10110	00110000	0000
1	10111	00110001	0001
2	10011	00110010	0010
3	00001	00110011	0011
4	01010	00110100	0100
5	10000	00110101	0101
6	10101	00110110	0110
7	00111	00110111	0111
8	00110	00111000	1000
9	11000	00111001	1001

Comparison of Baudot's 5-bit code, ascii 8-bit code and the binary number for the numerals 0–9. Numerals in Baudot's code would have to be preceded by a shift code of 11011.

decoding specific, albeit digital, German coded messages. So why was the world of computation and information processing all analogue at the end of the 1940s? Why did no one and none of these technologies anticipate the digital revolution? Well, some did, as we will find out later, but there are a number of reasons, one of which was certainly the unrivalled success of analogue computation and control mechanisms during the war.

One reason that analogue computing was so successful, as a computational system, was its speed. In fact, even today there is still active research into analogue computing because of its speed and accuracy in calculation (mathematical computation). The reason that analogue computing is, and was, so fast is because it does calculations directly. Now, this may seem both counterintuitive and confusing to most people, but let me explain a bit. When a digital computer does something simple like adding two numbers together, it is, in fact, performing a rather complicated procedure. First of all, a digital computer, despite what you have always been told, does not store numbers in binary. Though the digital codes for numbers, as we saw in Chapter Two, are binary, having only two states, they are not binary numbers. We can see this more clearly in the preceding table which compares Baudot's 5-bit digital code for numbers with the ASCII 8-bit digital code and binary numbers.

Though modern computers store numbers, and characters, as 32- or even 64-bit addresses for codes, these codes do not correspond to the binary numbers as numbers. So the first thing that a computer has to do before it even begins to add two numbers together is to translate the digital code for the numbers we enter into binary numbers.

Then you would think that a binary computer would simply add the two binary numbers together as we would:

0011	3
0101	5
1000	8

However, computers do not work with numbers like this. In fact, they do not compute in this sense at all, but, instead, process digitally encoded input, literally just a single electrical current being either on or off, through a series of logic gates. I am not going to bother you here with how logic gates work. This is a separate subject that is of interest to many, but whose specificities need not concern us here. However to add the two numbers above, a digital computer would need no fewer than four 'adders' consisting of four logic gates each. That is a total of sixteen logic gates to add these two numbers. Of course, at the end of the addition, the computer would again have to translate the binary number (1000) for 8 into its digital code (111000 for 8-bit ASCII, for example) so we could then read the result on the screen as an '8' – of course only after the computer had also gone through a large number of processes to actually render an '8' on the screen, in the right font and size, and in the right place.

Today, digital computers have vast quantities of transistors (logic gates) and can do this seemingly complex operation at extraordinarily fast speeds. However fast, though, they still have to do it at the speed of electrical transmission. They cannot go faster. And, in the past, digital computers didn't have anywhere near as many transistors (logic gates) as they do today. In the 1950s, and even in the 1960s, this was a serious limitation on the speed of calculation for digital computers. It was only by the 1970s and '80s that digital computer chips became large enough (and, ironically, small enough) to achieve truly large processing speeds and accuracies.[13]

For analogue computers, this speed problem did not exist. The reason was that analogue computers compute, literally add and subtract numbers, by merely increasing or decreasing the electrical current by the necessary amount or, as was the case early on, through the mechanical distance of cogs, wheels and shafts. The quantities being calculated in an analogue computer are analogous to actual distances that wheels or shafts move, or the actual quantities of electricity in a circuit. So if we were to solve the above addition problem with an electronic analogue computer, we would simply have a register of current that we could read, and then input 3 units of electricity followed by an increase of 5 units of electricity and instantaneously read the result of 8 units. To subtract we would just take the 8 units and decrease the current by 5 units and be back at our original 3 units, instantaneously.

Engineers in the 1940s, '50s and '60s had devised a staggering array of different electromechanical means by which to do everything from simple arithmetic to complex mathematical calculations, all at astonishingly fast speeds. It wasn't until the late 1950s that the sheer power of digital processing was able to begin to match that of analogue computers for mathematical calculations. Even today, there remain areas of research that are working with and developing analogue computers that cope with certain very complex computational problems that are simply too big for digital computers. Current problems of complex image processing, neural networks and Big Data analysis involve so many data points that we are reaching the limit of what digital computers can cope with – within reasonable time spans. There are problems today that use techniques, such as fast Fourier transforms, where, with the very large datasets we now have, a digital computer would need many hundreds of years to solve the problem. New analogue computers are being designed that could solve these huge mathematical problems in a few days or weeks, rather than after the hundreds of years that even current digital supercomputers would require.

So, if analogue computers are so good at computing, why are we not all using analogue computers? There are a number of reasons, some of which we will deal with in the next chapter. However, one major reason is that, from the earliest times to today, you cannot build an analogue computer that is 'universal'. What this means is that each analogue computer has to be designed to solve a single problem or a single kind of problem. We could say that the nineteenth century and the first half of the twentieth century was the age of analogue devices, but what you notice, if you look at the computational and information technologies from 1900 to 1950, is that there are lots and lots of different devices. Not just different brands of devices, as we have today, but lots and lots and lots of different devices, each one designed to solve a very particular problem.

What today we would characterize as data or information was recorded and stored differently then. It was either written down, mechanically inscribed, printed or typed out onto paper or some other medium. There were technologies, as we all know, for recording and storing sound (phonograph and audio tape), images (photographs) and moving images (film), as well as text (printing). The phonograph was invented in the 1870s and, as you will recall, Thomas Edison received his Grande Médaille d'Or for the phonograph at the same ceremony at which Baudot received his for his telegraph, in 1878. The phonograph had transformed music and speech, making whole genres of music widely available for the first time. Folk music and genres such as blues had rarely been heard outside their local heartlands because they were not written forms of music. Remote and distant parts of the world were now being accessed via photographs and film. We cannot overestimate the impact that the phonograph, photography and film had on society in the first half of the twentieth century as people, for the first time, could relatively rapidly witness events happening on the other side of the world, or in communities that were socially inaccessible. People could take photographs and have them developed to paper, and could, if they had enough money, 'shoot' films, offering a level of personal archiving of memories that today is pervasive, but then was unique. From the early days of television, there was also video recording, but this was, like the other technologies, firmly analogue. However, video technology then was really only available for corporate use as, in 1956, a bottom-of-the-line video recorder would set you back $50,000 (over fourteen times the average annual salary in the U.S. at the time), and a one-hour reel of videotape $300 (roughly the cost of a car at the time).[14]

What we find difficult to comprehend these days is how profoundly different all these different technologies were from each other. The way that you recorded sound, onto vinyl discs, was completely different from, and incompatible with, the way you recorded an image or even sound on film. Though there were similarities between the way the photographs were recorded, and the media they used, and film, the two technologies were significantly different. The way that television recorded moving images was influenced by film, but diverged radically from it in its technologies of recording, storage and transmission. The way that text and images were printed and stored was also substantively different from the technologies for image (still or moving) and sound recording. For all these media, you needed not only technologies to record, but quite separate technologies to portray and perform them.

Today, especially since about 2000, we are living in a world where information technology is distinguished by *convergence*. So what does this mean? Almost all our digital computers work in more or less the same way. Though there are many small differences between computer chips, their instruction sets and certainly between operating systems, all these digital devices work by the same basic set of processing principles and with very similar architecture. There are special-purpose chips for specific applications, but these too work by very similar principles. Add to this that our devices, because they are universal processors, can be used to emulate almost any systematic technological process; our current devices do the work that hundreds of devices did previously. When I was a young boy, more than half a century ago, we had not even seen a computer, though I had heard about them. We did, however, have telephones, TVs, radios, phonographs, telegrams, a letter post, magazines, newspapers, books and encyclopaedias around the house, as well as a local library. We also had cameras and tape recorders, and some neighbours even had movie cameras. There were also, in different businesses around our town, filing technologies, indexing systems for finding information, and computational technologies such as adding machines, cash registers, tabulation machines, sorters, ledger systems and so on. There were devices for measuring aspects of our environment and our bodies, such as thermometers, altimeters and compasses; and technologies for finding our way, such as maps, sextants and plane tables. We also had medical technologies for measuring heart rates and blood pressure. I could go on to list the analogue technologies for maintaining cars and other forms of transport, for the management of agriculture, for the measurement and prediction of the weather, for all areas of life and science. Today, however, I have all these technologies, in one form or another, bundled into a small flat device with a little screen that fits into my pocket. This is *convergence*.

As we can see from the long list above, convergence simply wasn't an option for analogue systems. If you needed to listen to sound, you had a phonograph or a magnetic tape player. If you wished to see moving images, there was film or, later, TV. Recording these moving images required either copying the film, or having access to another form of magnetic tape recording (videotape). If you wanted to do some addition or subtraction, you used one sort of device (an adding machine); if you wanted to multiply or divide, there was another device (a slide rule). You took photographs with one sort of camera and moving pictures with another sort. If you worked with large amounts of information or data – and many people did, even then – you had one set of machines to tabulate the information, another set to sort and yet another to search. This was not a very efficient way of working, yet it spawned a massive and global set of industries of which today's information industries are but mere extensions.

There are other problems with analogue technologies that we encountered in the last chapter. Analogue systems were divorced from data. Data lived in a different medium from analogue processing mechanisms, so it had to be physically transported, loaded and read into the devices. The results of the processing also had to be read and recorded. We saw, in the last chapter, how punched card technologies were initially used to store only the data for information processing, only the records of information. It was only later, in the early 1930s, that it was realized that punched cards could also be used to record the results of processed data from punched cards, but the processing continued to be through a plethora of analogue mechanisms.

Despite what today we would see as an obviously unnecessary complexity of machines and systems, throughout the first seventy years of the twentieth century analogue devices, processing and computation remained practically the only game in town. Only in the transmission of text – telegrams and telex – did digital reign supreme, albeit through electromechanical devices. However, we should not assume that the digital was simply waiting its turn to be appreciated as an obviously superior technology. Much had yet to happen for the digital to even begin to be applied as a universal medium, and none of what was to happen was at all self-evident or inevitable.

From analogues to digitals: electronic decision-making

In May 1936, a young Cambridge mathematician submitted a paper to the *Proceedings of the London Mathematical Society* entitled 'On Computable Numbers, with an Application to the *Entscheidungsproblem*'.[15] Alan Turing, who would become famous early in the war for building the Bombe, the analogue computer that broke the German Enigma code, had only just been appointed a Fellow of King's College straight from his undergraduate degree in mathematics. 'On Computable Numbers', written just before Turing went to work on his doctorate at Princeton University in the U.S., showed that there were many problems in mathematics that could be solved by a machine. However, not just any machine, but a machine that could operate in a systematic and logical way, algorithmically, the way that computers did. Of course, in 1936 Turing did not mean by *computers* the electronic devices we have today. As discussed before, computers (or computors) then were people who worked by algorithmically dissecting mathematical problems into a number of logical steps that could be solved in a distributed sequence. What Turing achieved was not a computer, but the principles for a universal computing device – what became known as the Universal Turing Machine or UTM.

The *Entscheidungsproblem* was a problem posed by the German mathematician David Hilbert in 1928. Hilbert asked if there were an algorithm that takes as its input a first-order logic statement and whose answer is 'Yes' or 'No' depending on whether the statement is universally true. Now this may be as clear as mud to most of us, but for mathematicians it was a keen challenge, and Alan Turing proved that there was no solution to the *Entscheidungsproblem*. More importantly, though, Turing proved that there was no algorithm that could solve the *Entscheidungsproblem*.

In the same year, 1936, an American mathematician and logician also published a paper proving that the *Entscheidungsproblem* could not be solved. Alonzo Church was a professor of mathematics at Princeton University, and it seems that neither Church nor Turing knew of the other's work. However, the serendipitous discovery by Church offered an ideal solution for Turing's problem of where to do his PhD. From September 1936 to July 1938 Turing spent most of his time working with Church in Princeton on his doctorate.

After his doctorate, Turing returned to Cambridge as a Fellow, but also began working part-time at the Government Code and Cypher School. This is what led to his being recruited for code-breaking work at Bletchley Park early in the war and his work to break the notorious Enigma code.

UTM: Universal Turing Machine

Though Turing is better known for his code-breaking work, and his infamous trial for homosexuality which may ultimately have led to his suicide, his 1936 article included a far more important revelation than the mere proof of the insolvability of the *Entscheidungsproblem*. Though Church also resolved the *Entscheidungsproblem* in a similar way to Turing, Turing went on to prove that you could design a machine that would be capable of performing any mathematical computation if you could represent it as an algorithm – 'computing machines'.[16]

Turing's Universal Turing Machine (UTM), as it was dubbed by Alonzo Church, was a conceptual model for a machine that was never intended to be built. Its purpose, for Turing, was to demonstrate that you could design a machine which could, in principle, solve all the mathematical problems that human computers could solve, as long as the problems could be represented as an algorithm. The UTM is often misrepresented as a machine that could, in principle, solve all computational problems. This is certainly not true, not least as Turing's paper proved that the Entscheidungsproblem, at least, was not solvable at all, and he also showed that there was a large class of mathematical problems that could not be solved by his machine.

The machine itself was extremely simple, you will be glad to hear. His conjectural machine consisted of a scanning head, and a 'limitless' paper tape divided into squares. Each square, which was editable and could be blank, would hold a single symbol from a finite symbol set, such as the alphabet. Contrary to many accounts of the UTM, Turing never suggested that this symbol set should be digital (or even binary), though he did show how his machine could easily accommodate binary computation. One of the key innovations of his machine was that the tape would operate as a universal memory, holding not only the sequence of instructions for the computer, but all the data for the computation and the output, since the tape was limitless and the squares could be written to, read and erased. What was proposed was a general-purpose storage medium which held both data and processing instructions.

The other key innovation of Turing's machine was that it would operate sequentially. The instructions (the program) and the data would be read off the paper tape and performed in sequence. As with today's computer programs, the idea was that, unlike the current analogue computers that operated as a coordinated whole to solve

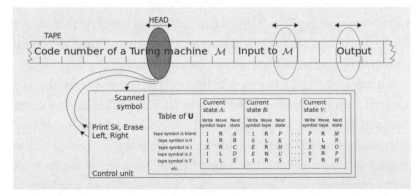

Model of how the Universal Turing Machine could have worked.

a single type of problem, Turing's computing machine would take a series of instructions, and perform them on a stored body of data, in sequence. The stored program, or algorithm, was for Turing a script that prescribed the process by which some problem would be solved performatively – literally *performing* the algorithm.

Turing also proposed for his machine that it would, uniquely for the time, have its own local set of basic instructions that would allow it to process the stored program. Instructions such as 'move one space to the right', 'write a symbol stored in this location' or 'erase the contents of the current square' would be the instructions for the basic operation of the machine rather than the program. This is what today we would call the operating system.

Turing's conceptual machine was designated as 'universal' because it could, in principle, be programmed to perform any calculation that could be performed by the human computers. The human computers used systematic, rule-based procedures that followed a fixed table of instructions – algorithms. Turing did not propose a machine that could calculate; he proposed a machine that could do algorithms. What Turing did was to propose a mechanism by which a fixed table of instructions could be given to a machine rather than a group of people. The UTM did this, Turing proposed, by encoding the instructions from the instruction table onto the paper tape. The first instruction would fill a specified number of squares on the tape, the second line of instructions would fill a second specified number of squares, and so on. This method Turing called the 'standard description' of the instruction table. All possible instruction tables could be, in principle, encoded onto the paper tape and be applied to any possible set of data also encoded onto the paper tape. The paper tape would act as the machine's memory for instructions, data and output, all using a set of basic instructions that would be 'hardwired' into the machine.

Turing went on to prove, mathematically, that such a machine was capable of carrying out every computation that can be encoded into an instruction table. However, he never mentioned, or even considered, at this time, how his 'computing machine' would actually operate.

There were no plans for a mechanism, no details of how the hard-wired instructions would be hardwired or even what they may all be. There were no particulars of how the information on the tape would be encoded, or how the machine would 'understand' this encoding. In fact, it was not at all clear, at the time, how one could go about starting to build such a machine.

In all fairness to Alan Turing, he was not really interested in such questions, at least not at that time. In his paper 'On Computable Numbers' Turing was interested in solving a problem in mathematical logic and showing, by presenting a conceivable machine, what kind of problems could be solved by algorithms (fixed instruction tables). He was later certainly interested in the practical problems of building such a machine, or something like it, and this interest would grow almost to an obsession at the end of his life in the early 1950s. However, it is important to understand that though Turing presented the conceptual design for a stored program computer, a computer that showed how machine memory could act to store not only the data and the output of computations, but the instructions for those calculations, this did not imply the digital computer, certainly not as we know it today. Turing's computing machine did not require digitality for the encoding, or for the logic processing. Like so many other computational technologies of the time, the importance, even the utility, of digital encoding and processing was not seen, certainly not as a necessity. It remained an analogue world of special-purpose mechanisms where even a sequential universal computing machine could be envisioned to be fully analogue. Though digital encoding existed, and had existed for over sixty years, a number of other developments were needed to elevate the digital to a dominant position as a fully integrated processing medium.

Relays and information theories

Vannevar Bush's Differential Analyzer at MIT was churning out computations throughout the 1930s. As one of the most important analogue analysers of the 1930s and early 1940s, Bush's later Rockefeller Differential Analyzer attracted engineers from all over the U.S. to work on it. One such young engineer was a recent graduate of the University of Michigan, Claude E. Shannon. Shannon came to MIT as a master's student in 1936 after completing two BAs at the University of Michigan, one in electrical engineering and one in mathematics. Shannon later said that he took up the position in Bush's lab at MIT after reading a postcard notice on a campus bulletin board. In addition to getting his MA, Shannon was one of the technicians responsible for setting up the Differential Analyzer for different problems brought by engineers, scientists or governmental departments.

As an engineer working directly on the Differential Analyzer, Shannon quickly gained an intimate knowledge of how the Analyzer worked, as well as the detailed workings, and problems, of its many parts. We have to remember that the Differential Analyzer was not a computer as we know it today. Today, even for programmers, the inner workings of the computer are never, or rarely, accessed directly. With today's distributed computing and Web services, even programmers rarely see the actual computer they are working on, which could be on another continent. For Shannon and his fellow engineers and technicians, this was an unimaginable situation. The computer they worked on was very immediate and required direct manipulation of all its parts for each and every problem they put to it.

So, working on the Differential Analyzer for Shannon meant not just moving the rods, motors and plugboards, but also caring for, maintaining and repairing the automated punched-tape access units, the 2,000 vacuum tubes, the 150 motors and several thousand relays. A relay is a very simple electrical switch which uses an electromagnet. When an electrical current turns on the electromagnet, it causes a metal switch to either close, closing another electrical circuit, or to open, opening another electrical circuit. The origin of these electrical switches is a bit obscure, but they were certainly invented by the 1830s for telegraphs. Samuel Morse's first patent included a plan for a relay. Relays are very useful not only because you can use one electrical circuit to open or close another, but because the electrical power going into the two circuits can be different. So, you can use a very low-voltage circuit to close a very high-voltage circuit, which is much safer. In fact, circuits are incredibly common today, and are used in almost all electrical and electronic systems. On the Differential Analyzer, the way that the relays were connected was one of the components that set the analyser up to solve a particular problem.

Claude Shannon was a diligent tinkerer, both with mechanisms and with ideas. He would later build many apparently useless, but clever, devices just for the fun of it. He built a Throbac (THrifty Roman-numerical BAckward-looking Computer), which was a Roman numeral calculator. He also built the 'Ultimate Machine', a box with a switch on the front. When you flipped the switch, the box would open and a mechanical hand would come out, turn the switch off and shut the lid. What Shannon liked doing was to reduce every problem to its most basic form and then attack it from an unusual angle.

In addition to working on the Differential Analyzer, Shannon also had to work on his MA thesis. He decided to work on the relays and on the problem of finding the simplest circuit representation of the network synthesis problem. If you recall from the beginning of the chapter, we discussed the importance of network analysis to both tele-communications and electrical distribution. Network analysers were some of the most important analogue computational devices of the early twentieth century, and the problem remains important for the analysis of problems up to the present day. Shannon wanted to find algorithms or a 'calculus' for determining the most efficient way of setting up the relays to solve problems on the Differential Analyzer, thus saving time and reducing error.

He did this in his MA thesis, 'A Symbolic Analysis of Relay and Switching Circuits', by first expressing the characteristics of the net-work as a series of equations, where the relays in the system were the characteristics. In the second step he reduced these equations to the simplest form. So he developed a 'calculus' using simple algebraic algorithms that provided a way of computing the simplest forms of circuits. In the end, the circuit for the problem could be drawn directly from the simplified equations. What Shannon did was to show how you could develop algorithms for solving problems using circuits of relay switches.

This was certainly a considerable achievement for an MA student, but this is not the reason that Shannon's is still referred to as the most important MA thesis of the twentieth century. Shannon brought a completely new and unique understanding to the working of these relays. He noticed that the calculus he had developed was almost identical to the Calculus of Propositions developed in the 1840s and '50s by the English mathematician George Boole.

Much can be said of George Boole as a mathematician. He was interested in and worked on the mathematics of differential equations, but is best known for his work on symbolic logic. Symbolic logic is a means of analysing logic, rational decision-making, via mathematics. What concerned Shannon was Boole's 'An Investigation of the Laws of Thought, on Which are Founded the Mathematical Theories of Logic and Probabilities', published in 1854. In this paper Boole outlined his algebra of logical relations. These are what today we know as the logical relations of UNION, INTERSECTION and NEGATION that we all learn in school. Basically, A and B, A or B and A not B. Boole's algebra, and its current form which has been built on and transformed, is much more complicated than just these three simple relationships, but this gives the basic idea of what Shannon noticed.

When Shannon noticed that his calculus was largely the same as the algebra of Boole, he recognized something that would become extremely important. He recognized that circuits, made up of relays (on and off switches), could be organized so that they could solve algorithms – that they could be programmed to make decisions. That the *ons* and *offs* of the relay circuits could be understood, in mathematical logic, as *trues* and *falses*.

The implications of this realization, a realization that no one else seems even to have anticipated, were enormous. As Shannon himself said, 'It is possible to perform complex mathematical operations by means of relay circuits.'[17] Aside from showing that such a system could add binary numbers, he went on to show how such logic circuits could make comparisons and make conditional decisions such as 'if the number X equals the number Y, then do operation A.' It is this quality of electrical switches, the ability to be used to do logic, which is the foundation of all electronic digital computers. What Shannon did in his MA thesis was nothing less than to show that we could build digital logic circuits – the digital chips in all our computers and digital devices. He not only suggested that we could build them, but showed us how we could do it. He even provided, at the end of his thesis, the diagram and description of a lock which could be opened and closed by switches and a binary logic circuit. Of course such locks are common today, but in 1937 it was a revolutionary revelation.

In an interview in 2001, Charles Vest, president of MIT from 1990 to 2004 and a friend of Claude Shannon later in his life, said that Shannon once told him that it just 'dawned' on him that the relay circuits of the Differential Analyzer he was assembling resembled the Boolean logic he had studied at Michigan as a BA student.[18] We could ask whether there would have been a digital revolution had the young Shannon not made this realization, and the answer would certainly be 'Yes.' However, it remains a question as to how long it would have taken if Shannon had not made this essential connection as, from the point of view of an historian, it was clear that no one was thinking along the lines of using switches to logically process information. Many people had been thinking for some time how to create mechanisms and machines that would calculate binary numbers, but not how to use integrated circuits of binary switches, switches that subjected to an input offered the output of either a true (on) or false (off), to solve logical problems – problems that involved making digital decisions.

After his master's, Shannon went on to do a PhD, with the encouragement of Vannevar Bush, in mathematical techniques applied to the new field of genetics. He managed to finish his PhD in a year and a half, but, owing to the fact that he never managed to publish its results in anything but an obscure genetics journal, his work had little impact on genetics. After his PhD, with the war now imminent, Shannon was recruited to Bell Labs to work on gun control systems and cryptography (codes and code-breaking). His work on code-breaking would have a deep impact on his work over the next few years.

Shannon's work on code-breaking centred mostly on the problem of redundancy in language. All languages have redundant bits, such as the u that always follows a q in English. The u is not necessary at all, but is always included. We do not necessarily need to use the word *the*, but we do as both a convention and to refine meaning. These are examples of redundancy.

For codes and code-breakers, redundancy is very important. It is important for code-breakers as it is the redundancy of language that allows them to find key patterns in a code so it can be broken. For code-makers, it is important to remove as much redundancy as possible to make the code unbreakable. Shannon wrote at the time, 'In . . . the majority of ciphers . . . it is only the existence of redundancy in the original messages that makes a solution possible.'[19] So, what Shannon argued was that a code that had less redundancy was harder to crack. More than that, what Shannon did with his work at Bell Labs was to be able to quantify how much redundancy needed to be removed from a message to make it unbreakable. He did this by associating the reduction of redundancy with the amount of 'noise' in a channel – the amount of interference on a communications channel that makes it hard to interpret the original message.

Those of us old enough to not only remember analogue telephones, but to have used them when the channels – the wires and exchanges – were rather poor, remember perfectly what is meant by noise. As a child growing up in India, in the 1960s, it was a constant challenge to understand what the other person was saying on the phone for the cracks, snaps, hisses and dropouts that were a constant hindrance. Trying to distinguish the other person's voice over the 'noise' was a challenge, and there was much 'Could you repeat that?', 'What was that?' and 'I missed that last bit.'

The relationship between redundancy, 'noise' and understanding a message became a major concern for Shannon during the war. As was usual for him, he sought to reduce the problem to its simplest form so he could characterize it algorithmically. His work was extremely influential on the Vernam System developed at the end of the war. The Vernam System used Shannon's mathematical abstraction to reduce redundancy in the message to almost 0, making it all but impossible to break the coded message. This system was presented in a classified report in 1946, 'A Mathematical Theory of Cryptography',[20] where Shannon developed a simplified model for such a coded message which reduces the problem of communication to a few simple components, such as the message source, the receiver, the channel, and agents that act on the message and channel.

Why should we be worried here about the wartime exploits of Claude Shannon, especially in cryptography? There is an important reason. A reason that had at least as much impact on the development of digital computing and digitality as did his master's thesis. While working at Bell Labs on cryptography, Shannon was also working, on his own, on the concept of 'information', or, as he originally characterized it, 'intelligence'. As early as 1939, Shannon wrote to Vannevar Bush that

Off and on I have been working on an analysis of some of the fundamental properties of general systems for the transmission of intelligence, including telephony, radio, television, telegraphy and so on. Practically all systems of communication may be thrown into the following general form:[21]

$$f_1(t) \rightarrow \boxed{T} \rightarrow F(t) \rightarrow \boxed{R} \rightarrow f_2(t)$$

'Information' had been an important problem since the beginning of the twentieth century. With the explosion of communications technologies, the issue of getting the message through had become critical, not only for governments, militaries and businesses, but for the growing population that relied on, and paid for, communication technologies. As early as 1924, a Bell Labs engineer, Harry Nyquist, had worked on the problem of 'Certain Factors Affecting Telegraph Speed', where he explored the factors affecting the 'speed of transmission of intelligence'.[22] By 'intelligence' he meant both the signal of a message, that which was transmitted, and the signal as received, as the same signal without distortion, but also what the meaning of the message was for a person. Nyquist did not distinguish between the signal transmitted and what is normally understood as the signal's meaning. Rather, his contribution was that he suggested that there could be an 'optimum code' that would allow the maximum amount of 'intelligence' transmitted over a line when the number of signal elements (letters, numbers, symbols) was known.

A few years later, in 1928, another Bell Labs engineer, R.V.L. Hartley, clarified Nyquist's ideas by arguing that, as an engineering problem, it was unnecessary to consider what the actual 'meaning' of a message was, but that what mattered was to determine how to transmit the message at the maximum speed with minimal distortion.[23]

> Hence in estimating the capacity of the physical system to transmit information we should ignore the question of interpretation, make each selection perfectly arbitrary, and base our results on the possibility of the receiver's distinguishing the result of selecting any one signal from that of selecting any other. By this means the psychological factors and their variations are eliminated and it becomes possible to set up definite quantitative measure considerations alone.[24]

Drawing on the work of both Nyquist and Hartley, Shannon worked throughout the war on generalizing these two insights – the optimum code and information transmission as a purely engineering problem – even further. He fully accepted Hartley's argument that information transmission, as an engineering problem, had nothing whatsoever to do with meaning. It is not that Shannon did not think that the meaning of a message, what we understand is meant or what is said, was unimportant – on the contrary. What he was interested in, however, was the engineering problem of how to get a signal, which consisted of a series of encoded symbols – which from the engineer's point of view only incidentally has meaning for a sender and a receiver – from a transmitter to a receiver without any errors in the symbol sequence. It was this signal of encoded symbols that he designated 'information'.

It seems that he had largely formulated his theory of information by 1943, but for some reason still unknown he didn't feel compelled to publish his findings during the war. However, he did publish his groundbreaking paper 'A Mathematical Theory of Communication' in 1948.[25] In his paper, Shannon showed how all the diverse forms of communication media could be combined and measured within a single mathematical theory of information as transmitted symbols. Building on the work of both Nyquist and Hartley, both of whom he referenced at the beginning of the paper, Shannon presented a theory of how you could determine how much information could, in all conditions, potentially be sent down a line.

Shannon's paper made four separate contributions to what would become information theory. First, he proposed a formal model of communications systems, a refinement of the one he presented in his cryptography paper. Second, he discussed the problem of 'source coding', how well you can represent a message even when you have removed the redundancy – what today we think of as data compression. Third, he formulated an algorithm for determining how much information can be, in theory, sent down a line – any line. Finally, and most important for us, he proposed and demonstrated the idea of digital representation, or digital encoding of all information, not just text.

For the first three revelations, any one of which would have been earth-shaking, Shannon proposed radically new and simple models, though the implications of these models would take decades to realize. He started by presenting a simplified model of information transmission. We must remember that what was most important, and revolutionary, about Shannon's model was not that it represented human communication, as others would go on to argue in the 1950s and '60s, but that it was required to model only the sending of a signal of encoded symbols down a channel, literally how can we best send electronic signals down a wire or by radio. By reducing his problem to this engineering problem, Shannon was able to solve some very difficult problems of data transmission and data processing.

The second and third contributions, of source coding and the association of information content with entropy, were truly revolutionary, and continue to have the greatest impact on our communication technologies today. Shannon demonstrated both that you could create a code that would optimally minimize the expected length of a signal, and that you could calculate the amount of information in the channel. The significance of the first was that Shannon showed not only that it was possible, but how you could compress data. All of our current methods for compressing digital data (JPEGs, MP3s, .ZIP files, even 3G and 4G signals for our phones) are the direct descendants of Shannon's theorems. The other contribution would offer a solution to the problem of sending lots of data as a signal. The standard solution at the time was to use a narrow bandwidth with lots of energy. This was the solution of radio and television, and was a method enforced by law as these narrow bandwidths were licensed by the government. What Shannon showed was that you could choose. You could send your data over a narrow bandwidth with lots of energy, or you could also send the same amount of information, just as efficiently, over a wide bandwidth with low energy – like broadband. Though the computational algorithms for doing this are complex, this ultimately opened up the possibility for all the mobile communications we have today. Your mobile smartphone is a device that makes direct use of Shannon's principles of wide bandwidth and low energy, as does your Wi-Fi.

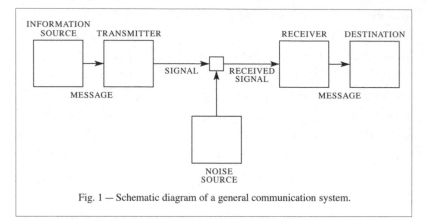

Fig. 1 — Schematic diagram of a general communication system.

Shannon's Information Model, from his article 'A Mathematical Theory of Communication', 1948.

These principles would also give rise to a new field called information science. Though the field would go through many ups and downs, mostly due to, in the early years, the lack of technology powerful enough to drive the consequences of these theories, it would revolutionize communications technology, ultimately giving us the Internet and mobile communications. However, there was a fourth achievement that interests us here. Drawing from his work on cryptography, Shannon argued that the randomness and redundancy of a signal is dependent on the number of symbols that make up the message. This he associated with the concept of entropy, or randomness in a system. Shannon showed how the entropy was low, low randomness, in a signal if the symbol set used to encode the contents was small (used very few characters or symbols), and that the signal would be very random, high entropy, if the symbol set was large. Simply put, if you have a large symbol set – say the English alphabet and numerals, 36 symbols in all – it is difficult for the receiver to determine which symbol is which, over a transmission channel which may be noisy, as the number of choices is very large. However, if you have a small symbol set, say a digital 1 or 0, then the ability of the receiver to determine the symbol is greater as there are only two possibilities. By showing this direct relationship between the number of symbols used to transmit a message and the randomness of the signal, Shannon showed not only that all transmission media could be treated the same way, but that all information, from any source, could be represented by the simplest information unit – 1s and 0s, digitally.

This efficiency of transmission was coupled, in Shannon's paper, with the concept that the information transmitted simply referred to the encoding symbols used. What this meant was that if you used the most efficient encoding symbols, 1s and 0s, digital encoding, 'bits' as Shannon coined the term in his paper, not only could the data be transmitted and regenerated without error, but the content of the message was irrelevant.

Let us stop for a moment and consider just what this means. Before Shannon's revelations, engineers and scientists thought of communications and computation as separate, discrete problems of analogue processing. If you had to send a message by telegraph or voice using a telephone, you would send electricity down the wire as bursts or you would modulate the electromagnetic waveform. If you needed to do a calculation, you would set up a machine that translated, by analogy, the quantities and their relationships into coordinated distances or time spans. The engineering and technologies for photography, for film, for telegraphy, for telephones, for radio, for computation, for measurement, for navigation all were separate domains. What Shannon realized was that if the content of the message was irrelevant for its transmission, storage and processing, then what the message represented or its mode of representation did not matter at all. For Shannon's theory, text, sound, image, video, measurements, maps and plans as vector data, and so on, did not matter. Any and all of these forms of information could be digitally encoded and transmitted, without error – as long as they were all encoded the same. The medium may be the message, but Shannon showed that you could create a technology that didn't need to care in the least about the message. More importantly, that technology needed to be digital.

This revelation came as a shock to the engineering community, and even to Shannon himself. His theory of information showed that any message, transmitted electrically, could be transmitted without error, especially if it was encoded as digital information. We take for granted today that we can listen to music, speak to our friends and colleagues, watch a movie or TV, write an email or a document, view a picture or perform any number of media interactions on a single device using digital information. However, in 1948, all of these analogue information systems were separate, not only mechanically and in terms of how they were inscribed, or in how they were replayed, but conceptually. No one thought that these different forms of information – sound, image, film, text, data – could be unified in a single theory, let alone encoded into a single medium. As Oliver Selfridge, an MIT graduate student at the time, said, 'It was a revelation . . . Around MIT the reaction was, "Brilliant! Why didn't I think of that?"'

These theorems and theories may seem like obscure mathematical curiosities only of use to engineers. For a long time, these 'information theories' were mostly just that, obscure engineering problems. By the end of the 1960s, information engineers heralded the end of the discipline, as they thought, then, that they could go no further as the technologies were not powerful enough to solve the error-checking problems that Shannon's algorithms proposed. They were wrong, as most of them were not aware of the callow industry of microprocessing that was just beginning to explode. Microprocessors, designed along Shannon's switching logic, would provide the processing power to solve the compression and error-checking computations. So successfully, in fact, that by 2001 we reached Shannon's predicted capacity for white Gaussian noise channels. It wasn't until a couple of decades after the first mass-produced microprocessors, in the early 1970s, that the technological problems of mass, wideband, mobile communications were sufficiently overcome for most of the world's population to have a mobile media device in their pockets.

Shannon did not build, nor did he even suggest that we should build, a digital computer. He did not create a way to encode digital images, digital video or even digital text. Baudot had shown how we could encode text as a digital code almost eighty years before

Shannon published his article. As we saw in the last chapter, by the time Shannon was working on his information theory, almost all electrically transmitted text, using telegraph and telex, had been digital for more than thirty years. Just as Turing had shown that it was possible to create a machine that could compute or process information any way people could, Shannon showed that it was possible to digitally encode anything that we could produce through any medium.

What is important to realize about Shannon's rarefied and mathematical characterization of information is that it demonstrated the possibility for all the digital technologies we live with today. How is it possible for us to read and write any form of text and image, to take and view photographs, to make and view video, to monitor any number of systems from personal health, to weather, to geography, to news, all on a single device? How is it possible for us to be able to abuse our CDs and DVDs by dropping them, getting our fingers all over them and spilling coffee on them, yet they still will play? How is it possible for us to send an email to a friend on the other side of the world, or even just down the street, transmitting the digitally encoded information through a series of points with fully effective error checking and recombination, even though these emails go down a variety of channels, copper wire, fibre optic cable, through the complex circuitry of your computer, the many servers and routers, to be reassembled, with perfect fidelity, on your friend's computer? Because all our digital computers, mobile phones, MP3 players, Internet servers and routers, digital cameras, smart gadgets and the entire world of digital devices work, fundamentally, on the digital principles laid out in Shannon's 1948 paper.

The very workings of our laptops and mobile phones depend on the principles of information transmission that Shannon demonstrated was possible. The vast amount of data being transmitted around your computer, from your hard disk, to your processor, through your motherboard, to your screen driver, to your screen; from your keyboard or microphone, back to your processor, to your memory, and back and forth and around all the hundreds of components that make up your laptop and the thousands of transmission channels all running at full speed without error. Components may fail, programs almost always have bugs, but all the information moves and arrives as it left, without error, because Claude Shannon managed to think of information simply as encoded digital bits, and opened the vast possibilities that this implied.

4
BACK TO CONTENT: FROM COMPUTATION TO MEDIA

The first computers, whether digital or analogue, were designed for a specific purpose or a set of related purposes. Like the earlier tabulating machines and electromechanical analysers, computers were largely designed to solve mathematical problems. As we discussed in the last chapter, computers were called computers because, as Alan Turing declared, these machines were to replace the work of human computors. As we have also seen throughout this story, the calculations of human computors were extremely diverse, supporting industrial, economic, military and governmental processes. It is for this reason, the need for computation, that computers remained largely analogue throughout the 1940s and '50s as digital processing couldn't compete sufficiently for computational speed with its analogue siblings. However, from a very early date, it was realized that the potential of digital computers to process logical programs, rather than just compute, and to be able to store vast quantities of information, which analogue computers could not do at all, offered new possibilities for human–computer interaction. It was the ability of the digital processor to literally make decisions, over vast quantities of digitally encoded information, that offered a whole new set of possibilities.

Decision-making machines had been around for a long time. From the early nineteenth century, governors in steam engines would mechanically 'decide' when to release pressure to avoid steam tanks breaking or even exploding. This was literally a mechanical decision-making system: too much pressure, open; too little, keep closed. Servomechanisms, such as the steam governor, have been a fundamental part of mechanical engineering for the past 200 years at least. The technological developments of the Second World War are seen as the epitome of servomechanism development, with much of the research effort on both sides dedicated to the development of mechanical or electromechanical servomechanisms – or servos, as they were called. Electrical relays were also a simple form of servo. Depending on the type of relay, which certainly existed prior to the first documented version in Samuel Morse's first telegraph patent, it would 'decide' to close or open a circuit when power was applied to the coil.

This is exactly what a computer transistor does, which is what Shannon realized when he noticed that as relays used electricity for their input and output, you could use the output of one relay as the input of another, thus creating assemblages of relays that could do mathematical logic – literally make systematic decisions. What this realization did was to recognize that the real power of these assemblages of relays (now transistors) was that they could process content using mathematical logic, as long as you could represent the content as a digital code.

It is surprising, not least as it is rarely acknowledged, how quickly content processing, information processing and programming – in fact, the creation of programs of action that augment human action – became the driving force for the development of digital computing. It is this return to content and augmentation of human action that we are concerned with in this chapter.

Error checking, visualization and interaction

There was an electrical device that was found in almost every home from the 1960s to just a few years ago. This device was an invention of the nineteenth century, but it did not find a practical or widespread application until just before and just after the Second World War. It was a device that initially had no practical application with computers, but would very quickly change the course of how computers were used, and what they were used for. This device was the cathode ray tube.

For those of you who never knew you were watching a cathode ray tube (CRT), or for those of you too young to remember having this type of TV in your home, a CRT was that very large glass tube that filled most of the large box that was a family TV, or your early computer monitor, back before we had LCD and LED flat screens. It was the tube that both projected the scanned image, as directed streams of electrons, onto a phosphor glass that you looked at to see your TV show or work on your computer. You can still find CRTs in many parts of the world, or even households (we only got rid of our 26-inch CRT TV a couple of years ago). There are still desktop computers with CRT monitors attached, though they are increasingly rare. My mother insists that she will not give up her desktop PC with CRT monitor attached. The room in which I am writing this bit of the book right now, somewhere in Italy, has an antiquated-looking 14-inch CRT TV in it, though I am not sure if it actually works. One wonders when these CRTs will find their way into bric-a-brac cabinets as 'antiques' of a bygone age. However, not very long ago CRTs were the dominant display technology in the world.

Though there have been flat-screen displays, for both TV and computer work, since the mid-1960s, and certain flat-screen displays such as LCDs have been on our devices since the late 1970s, it wasn't until about 2003 that flat screens began to completely replace CRTs, with CRTs all but disappearing from the market by 2009. From the 1950s to the early 2000s, however, the CRT was the display technology for both television and monitors.

When its explosion as a general entertainment instrument began in the 1930s, the CRT had already been around for some time. The basic principles that underlay its ability to project an image onto the inside of a glass tube coated with phosphors were laid down in the second half of the nineteenth century. Effective vacuum tubes were perfected in the 1850s and '60s, while the German physicist Julius Plücker experimented with what were then invisible 'cathode rays' at the same time. However, it was the Englishman William Crookes who was the first person to confirm the existence of cathode rays by displaying them on his Crookes tube.

William Crookes was experimenting with cathode rays, using vacuum tubes at the same time that Baudot was developing his code, in the early 1870s. By 1875, Crookes had developed a T tube (a T-shaped CRT called the Crookes tube) that was a partial vacuum tube with a phosphor coating at one end. Using high voltage between a cathode and an anode, at the other end, he could make the phosphors glow. The cathode is an electrode where electrically charged particles leave; the anode is where they arrive. On a typical battery, the cathode is the positive and the anode is the negative side. By putting a metal shape in the tube, there would be a clear shadow of the shape on the phosphors, demonstrating that the rays were travelling in a straight line. Later, the English physicist J. J. Thompson would identify the 'rays' as being streams of charged electrons that could travel through the partial vacuum in a straight line without hitting an air molecule.

Experimenting with his tube, Crookes and others found that by adding positively charged magnets at right angles to the cathode rays, they could deflect the rays within the tube by varying the strength of the magnetic charge. By placing two magnets just beyond the anode, perpendicular to each other, it was possible to direct a cathode ray beam to just about anywhere on the phosphor screen that you wished. It was this simple discovery, of the ability not only to create a beam of electrons that lit up a phosphor screen, but to direct a beam to any position on the screen, that made the CRT one of the twentieth century's most important display technologies, and that would ultimately make it an ideal display technology for digital media.

Another scientist, Karl Ferdinand Braun, was just beginning his career in the 1870s working on the properties of a set of metals which acted as electrical semiconductors, a technology that had no practical application at all in the nineteenth century, but that would become essential for the development of all semiconductor transistors used in computers from the 1950s onwards. Braun, along with Guglielmo Marconi, would later be awarded the Nobel Prize for key developments of another important communications medium of the twentieth century, radio. However, in 1897, Braun developed a working CRT that would take its input as a variable electrical signal, thus creating the first cathode ray oscilloscope. It was the ability of the Braun tube to systematically control the beam to produce an image on the screen that directly led to the development of television. In fact, in some countries, the television is still known as the Braun tube (in Germany it is known as the *Braunsche Röhre* and in Japan as the *Buraun-kan*).

It is interesting that, at the end of the nineteenth century, the original devices that attempted to transmit images electrically over a distance were called 'electrical telescopes', as they sought to bring distant images close. Other terms were also used, such as *télectroscope* and *Fernsehen*. However, it was in a lecture given by a Russian physicist, Constantin Perskyi, at the 1900 Paris Exhibition that these nascent technologies were termed 'télévision'. It seems that it was this designation which stuck for most European languages.

In June 1908 a pioneer of television technologies, Alan Archibald Campbell-Swinton, published a brief letter in the leading scientific journal *Nature*. In this letter, he suggested that a fully functioning television system could be built using a CRT as both the imaging system (camera) and the display. He also mentioned that he knew of 'No photoelectric phenomenon' in existence at that time that could provide the reception medium for the image; literally he knew of no mechanism that would detect the cathode rays as an image and transmit them. However, Campbell-Swinton had shown that if such a receptor could be found, such a system would work. Many took up his suggestion.

One of the people who turned their attention to this possibility was Vladimir Zworykin, a Russian émigré in the United States who had been working as a research engineer for the Westinghouse corporation since 1920. Working at Westinghouse gave Zworykin the time and resources he needed to develop his ideas for a CRT image capture and display system. As Campbell-Swinton had suggested, the problem was how to capture the image electronically. Zworykin achieved this by creating what he called the 'mosaic'. The mosaic was a surface that was basically a light-receptive grid that translated the light hitting each cell into an electric current that could be transmitted, much like your digital camera. More light on an individual point of the surface, more electricity at that point. As it was already well known how to direct the cathode rays within a CRT, rapidly, Zworykin's CRT device, which he called the iconoscope, could scan across and down the mosaic, in 512 lines, and read off the electrical charge at individual spots, today called pixels, 24 times a second. The light intensity of each spot was recorded by the cathode ray beam and converted into an analogue electrical signal, a signal very like a radio signal for sound. Zworykin also created a receiver for his signal which he called the kinescope. I am not going to go into great detail here about how Zworykin's iconoscope and kinescope worked,[1] nor is it of great interest to us here how Westinghouse showed little interest in the invention, prompting Zworykin to sell it to the leading radio and record company of the day, RCA. The development of Zworykin's system at RCA, and its parallel development by the BBC in the UK, is a fascinating history of technological rivalries and intrigues which laid the foundations for television to become the corporate broadcast medium of the twentieth century.[2]

What is of critical interest to us here is how Zworykin's iconoscope and kinescope allowed not only for the development of an analogue television industry, but for the possibility of first storing and then displaying digitally encoded data, thus also allowing for the development of digital information as a medium.

Vector rendering and raster bitmaps

Before we can discuss the impact of the screen, or the monitor, on early digital computing, we need to have a brief discussion about the different ways in which an image can be produced on a CRT. This is important because, today, there is really only one way that displays display. This was not always the case. In fact, until the advent of digital

TV, almost all televisions displayed their images in an analogue way. This is why, if you are old enough to remember, we had to either change our television, or get a translating box, when TV shifted to digital. The old TVs could not receive or display a digital signal because they worked in an analogue way.

As we discussed above with the development of the CRT, television displayed an image by scanning a light-sensitive layer and transmitting a variable signal that would render this scan onto the receiving screen, thus causing the phosphors on that screen to glow in the same intensity, and later the same colour, as the original signal. This was not a digital signal being created from a digital receptor, as our current digital cameras and videos work, nor was it processing a digital code that was then processed to make an LED glow in a certain way on our screens, as our current screens on all our devices do, but it was an analogue signal transmitted and received more in common with an FM radio signal.

Though this form of image transmission, that of analogue TV, dominated transmissions into our homes, computers always interacted with CRTs differently. Digital computers from the late 1960s mapped images, text and graphics onto a screen by treating all of these as a bit-image, broken down into thousands of little dots. This is the way that all display devices work today, by creating 'raster' bitmaps of very high resolution, so you don't see the dots but just the continuous image.

In the early days of personal computing, when most of us did see the dots, there was much kudos to be gained from having a 'higher-resolution' CRT – one that displayed these images more clearly. Today our devices have 'retinal displays', displays whose resolution is as fine as our eyes can detect, so we rarely think of 'resolution', but the resolution of a display was of great importance early on. This was not only because the quality of the picture was significantly affected by poor resolution, but because the early computers could not store, or effectively process, the large amounts of data that a high-resolution raster image requires. For this reason, the first CRT displays on computers did not use raster displays, but another way of displaying information – vector display.

Vector displays literally 'drew' the lines directly onto the screen, from one point to the next. Vector screens need much less data and processing as they simply store the start and end points of lines, which are then 'drawn' on the screen. Despite these technical differences, it was the first use of CRTs attached to computers as drawing devices that would quickly change the perceived *purpose* of the digital computer.

CRTs and computer storage

In the years just after the war, in the late 1940s, one of the problems for the early digital computers was the storage of data; not the storage of large, or even small, datasets, but the storage of digital information that needed to be held for a short time during the running of a program. During the past fifty years, this has been no problem at all as our computers store this data in dynamic memory that is either magnetic or electronic (the necessary RAM in your devices). However, for early computers, there was no storage technology which allowed them to write to, and read from, the memory fast. They could store this working data on paper tape, or even punched cards, but the time required to print the data and read it back would slow the program down so much as to make it unusable.

A very successful solution was developed in 1946 by two English engineers, Frederic Williams and Tom Kilburn. Frederic Williams was the Chair of Electrotechnics at the University of Manchester and he recruited Kilburn to work on what would become known as the 'Manchester Baby', one of the first successful digital computers. Williams and Kilburn found a practical solution to short-term memory in the then rather plentiful supply of wartime radar screens. The Williams–Kilburn tube storage solved the problem of rapidly writing and reading digital numbers by using the electrical charge that persists for a short time on the phosphors of a CRT screen. What they did was literally draw the binary numbers onto the CRT screen. As these would persist for short periods of time, but long enough for the computer processing, they could then read these stored points back as digital code when needed.

Of course they did not actually print '1's and '0's on the screen, but, interestingly, they did not do what we do today, which is to partition up the storage into 'locations' that either have a charge (corresponding to a 1) or do not have a charge (corresponding to a 0). Rather they used dots and dashes, much like Morse's code, with the dashes standing for 1s and the dots for 0s.

Though other forms of memory were also used, such as the highly toxic mercury delay tubes used for the early University of Cambridge computers, what today seems to us to be a very unconventional use of a CRT for computers was employed extensively as short-term, random access memory (RAM) not only for the early Manchester Baby, but for many other early digital computers. However, far more influential would be the extension of this idea to monitoring the computer itself, which happened surprisingly quickly.

Whirlwind 1

As we discussed above, servomechanisms were the technology of the Second World War. One of the leading research centres for servomechanisms was the Servomechanisms Laboratory at MIT in the United States. During the war, the servomechanisms lab worked primarily for the U.S. Navy, and the Navy approached the lab with the idea of creating an electronic computer that could drive a flight simulator to train bomber crews. Originally, the plan was modest, seeking only to have the computer simulate the outputs onto an instrument panel depending on the inputs from the trainee pilots. The advantage of its being computer-driven would be that it could easily be changed for different types of plane, since at the end of the war new planes were being developed and introduced rapidly. After the lab assessed that such a project was possible, Project Whirlwind, as it was known, was authorized.

In 1944, the project team rapidly built an analogue computer for the task, but it proved to be far too inflexible and inaccurate for the flight simulator. In 1945, a new recruit to the project, an engineer named Perry Crawford, saw a classified demonstration of the ENIAC (Electronic Numerical Integrator and Calculator), the U.S. military's new digital, or rather hybrid analogue/digital, computer, designed primarily for calculating ballistics and firing tables for artillery and bombing. However, as the ENIAC was at least partially digital – in that it used vacuum tube relays, though other bits were analogue and it was not programmed in the sense we know today – it was very fast. Crawford recognized that its speed and flexibility might be just what Project Whirlwind needed.

However, up to this point, all computers, even the very few digital ones, were built to perform a single task. In ENIAC's case it was to calculate, to do arithmetic, for ballistics. Whirlwind was to be something else, something more general-purpose, something that would have to perform logical algorithms, as suggested nine years before by Turing and Shannon. Whirlwind would not need to solve one problem at a time, like all computers up to that point, but would solve a number of problems all at the same time. So Whirlwind did not just have to be fast, it also had to be able to do a number of different things all at the same time, in parallel. This had never been imagined before, let alone achieved.

Although the war ended before the project was complete, the need remained, and by 1947 the Whirlwind team at MIT had a design for a digital computer that they felt would work. Now they had to build it. The lab began construction of what would be known as Whirlwind I in 1948. It took three years and the work of 175 people, of whom seventy were technicians and engineers. The resulting computer included a large number of innovations which would influence the development of computers to the present day.

The main problem for the Whirlwind team was to get the computer to do many things all at once. As computers continued to be considered single-task machines, such a problem had never been considered before. However, the MIT team quickly realized that instead of having one processing unit, a large unit of vacuum tubes doing the digital logic processing – what today we call the 'processor' – they could have a number of these working in parallel. All of your digital devices, from your laptop, to your phone, to your iPad, or even your TV or toaster, can do all the things they have to do – perform all the processes they have to perform all at the same time – because their binary processors, built onto their chips, work in parallel. It was here, with what seemed a simple problem for a flight simulator at the end of the 1940s, that this way of computing was created.

Another big problem for the team was that earlier digital computers used single-bit arithmetic with very long digitally encoded 'words' (or codes for numbers and/or letters). The MIT team saw that these long words would slow down the parallel processing of Whirlwind, and realized that because their core memory only needed so many places, they only needed 11 bits to tell the computer what the memory address would be, and an additional 5 bits for the digital code of the number or letter (from the Baudot–Murray code). So they determined, and implemented, a 16-bit 'word' length, which was the predominant encoding length up to the 1990s. All of our digital information today is recorded as individual, fixed length encodings that have their origins in this 16-bit method of encoding.

The Whirlwind team also had to produce a fast and workable core memory to hold these 16-bit 'words' to be used by the parallel processors. They first considered the standard mercury delay tubes, but quickly realized that these were far too slow, so they were quickly abandoned. They initially opted for the Williams Tube CRT storage, but instead of the well-developed Williams Tube they adopted another local version developed by the MIT Radiation Laboratory. However, this tube also proved to be far too slow and unreliable, so the project director, Jay Forrester, was forced to look around for other, more innovative options. In 1949, Forrester saw an advertisement for a new magnetic material that he felt could solve their problem. By linking rings of this material in a grid of wires, Forrester recognized that he could store 32 bits of memory on a single grid with very fast access. He gave the project to one of his master's students, Dudley Allen Buck, who quickly developed the magnetic core memory. Magnetic core memory would be the dominant form of RAM in computers until the advent of dynamic random access memory in the 1970s, which stores each individual bit on a separate capacitor in an integrated circuit.

However, from our point of view, the most important innovation of Project Whirlwind was not actually intended, or perceived as needed, but was, as is often the case, the unintended outcome of solving another problem.

In a speech in 1989, Norman Taylor, one of the engineers working on Project Whirlwind, talked extensively about how they used a CRT to monitor the operation of the individual vacuum tubes.

> When I was first called by Jan Hurst, she gave me an assignment to review the first 10 years of displays from '47 to '57 – and do it in 20 minutes. As I hung up the phone, the television showed President Bush talking about 1,000 points of light. All I could think of was, with due respect President Bush, we had 1,024 points of light in 1949.[3]

What Taylor was referring to here was a program they created, and which they called the 'Waves of One', that ran through the vacuum tubes checking to see if they got a response or not. If they did, there would be a dot on the screen for that vacuum tube; if not, it would be blank.

The problem that Taylor and his colleagues were trying to solve was to be able to find out quickly which vacuum tube had failed, as vacuum tubes failed frequently. The time needed to find and replace a failed vacuum tube was a major drain on program performance for all computers of the day. As time was project-critical for Whirlwind, the ability to find a failed tube, and know exactly where it was, saved a lot of time. This simple graphical representation of vacuum tubes – dots for good ones, blanks for failed ones – constituted the very first computer graphic. This was a bitmap of a condition in the computer generated by a program, not at all unlike your current CPU or Wi-Fi meter. But it is important to realize that this was 1948 and was the first time anyone had attached a CRT to a computer to *display* the output of a program.

The idea had already been suggested by John von Neumann in a memorandum in 1945. Von Neumann had suggested that

> In many cases the output really desired is not digital (presumably printed) but pictorial (graphed). In such situations the machine should graph it directly, especially because graphing can be done electronically and hence more quickly than printing. The natural output in such a case is an oscilloscope, i.e. a picture on its florescent screen. In some cases these pictures are wanted for permanent storage (i.e. they should be photographed); in others only visual inspection is desired. Both alternatives should be provided for.[4]

However, this memorandum was not widely circulated, so the idea was not acted on. There is no evidence that anyone at MIT knew of von Neumann's suggestion.

Though the Waves of One gave a graphical representation of which vacuum tube had failed, it did not give a representation of where it was in the computer. Like today, if we are getting a 'map' of our hard-disk storage, it is not an actual map of the hard disk, but a diagram of the disk. The Waves of One too was a diagram, so they needed some way of 'reading' from a dot, or more importantly from the absence of a dot, the information about where that was. According to Taylor, while they were considering how to address that spot on the screen, their technical director, Bob Everett, said:

> 'we can do that easily'. All we need is a light gun to put over the spot that stops and we'll get a readout as to which one it is. So he invented the light gun that afternoon and the next day we achieved man machine interactive control of the display – I believe for the

first time. This was late '48 or early '49. The next slide is a picture of one of those very early light guns.[5]

This very first light-gun, like our touch screens today, was a device that allowed the user to interact with the computer through a display – but this was in 1948. The idea that you could actually interact with a computer, graphically, had never before been considered as a need, let alone a possibility. These engineers – the first to build a fully parallel digital computer; the first to build magnetic core memory; the first to define 16-bit character sets that would work on a digital computer, rather than just act as a character code; the first to create a graphical interface to the computer – were also the first to design and implement a device that would directly interact with the computer. For a team working in a world with only a handful of computers, none of which had been around for more than six years, this was astounding.

The light-pen (or as the first version was called, the light-cannon) could not only read a dot on the screen and, using a program, retrieve

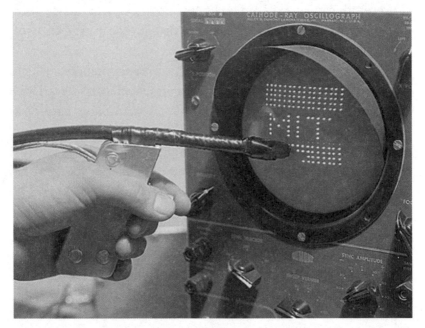

The Whirlwind CRT with an early light-pen displaying the MIT logo.

the location of that tube, but it could also directly interact with the CRT, drawing dots and lines, or even erasing bits. The potential of this was immediately recognized by the Whirlwind team when they began erasing dots from the Waves of One grid creating the MIT logo. When in 1951 the famous newscaster Edward R. Murrow interviewed the team for CBS News, Whirlwind displayed on its screen the words 'Welcome Mr. Murrow'.

Two years before Murrow's visit, in 1948 and 1949, almost immediately after Taylor and his colleagues wrote 'MIT' on their screen using the new light-pen ('light-cannon'), the 'mathematicians' displayed a few 'curves' on a small test CRT. According to Taylor, Charlie Adams, the original programmer of Waves of One, created a small bouncing ball game. Later, with the help of Jack Gilmore, they extended the bouncing ball so it would 'bounce' across the screen and, by changing a few parameters, you could get the ball to bounce into a hole on the lower right of the screen.

It seems to have been Adams who also first suggested that you could program a computer using a readable language, what today we call *coding*. In 1952, at the Association of Computing Machinery conference, Adams suggested that,

> Ideally, one would like a procedure in which the mathematical formulation together with the initial conditions can simply be set down in words and symbols and then solved directly by a computer without further programming.[6]

Soon, by 1950, the engineers and students at MIT were using Whirlwind and its interactive screen to graphically model all sorts of problems. Everything from the patterning of arrays of antennas, to modelling bomb drop trajectories, to modelling the path of a missile against its velocity and its fuel consumption (which was demonstrated to Murrow in 1951), all displayed graphically on their small screen. By this time, the Servomechanisms Laboratory, now renamed the Lincoln Laboratory at MIT, had given up working on servomechanisms and was no longer developing a flight simulator. However, the U.S. Air Force, the Federal Aviation Administration and the Air Defense Command had contracted MIT to develop Whirlwind into an air defence system. In conjunction with IBM, this is what became SAGE (Semi-Automatic Ground Environment), the USA's first fully automated and interactive air defence system which used interactive, on-screen graphics with light-pens updated over a complex digital network linking radar stations to an extensive network of monitoring stations, all by 1954.

After-effects and aftershocks: digitality as digital media

In part due to the success of the digital work at the Lincoln Lab, but also because the speed, real-time processing and flexibility of digital computing had become all too apparent, work on digital computing advanced apace around the world. Beyond ENIAC there were digital computers, or computer projects, at universities in California, Pennsylvania and even in Minnesota before the end of the 1940s. The U.S. government had digital computer projects for the military – many – but also for the National Census Bureau, the National Bureau of Standards and the Social Security system. In Britain the Manchester Baby had developed into the Manchester Mark 1, which was developed into Ferranti Mark 1, by 1951 the world's first commercially available computer. There was also Cambridge University's EDSAC computer. A number of companies were getting into the digital computer market: not only IBM, but Sperry Rand, Ferranti in Italy, Hewlett-Packard – even the British tea shop company J. Lyons and Co built their own LEO 1 computer in 1951. Though special-purpose analogue computers continued to dominate computing in the 1950s, digital computing was definitely growing, and growing rapidly.

With the extensive experience of Whirlwind, MIT set up its Advanced Computer Research Group in 1955. Headed by William Papian, they had separate teams responsible for software and logical design, and circuitry and computer production. Their first project was the TX-0 (Transistorized Experimental computer Zero), the world's first computer using only the new transistor circuitry, rather than vacuum tubes.

Aside from being the first fully transistorized digital computer, the TX-0 was an extension of the Project Whirlwind computer in most respects. It also used parallel processing and core memory and was interactive. However, with the TX-0, all these developments would be vastly extended. Though the TX-0 had less core memory than your credit card, it was nonetheless the fastest, most advanced and most powerful computer in the world in 1957. It would also go on to be the platform for a number of significant developments.

Early on in the TX-0 project, Jack Gilmore, one of the original engineers on Project Whirlwind, used the now standard computer interface used at MIT, the CRT display with a keyboard and light-pen, to build a program in 1956 that would help programmers debug programs using graphical flow charts with logical connections that could be opened and closed on the screen with the light-pen. Gilmore would go on to build the first text and graphics editor, the MIT Lincoln Writer. Using a full set of bitmapped characters and scientific symbols, scientists could model scientific problems graphically on screen and see the output. The need to actually write on the screen was so obvious that Gilmore created 'Scopewriter' in 1957, where he sought to emulate the working of a typewriter. In 1988, Gilmore would recall that

> what I believe the TX-0 really contributed was an online interactive man machine communication environment. We didn't really think about the fact that we were doing anything particularly impressive in the area of graphics, but we were trying to switch from a batch processing orientation to an interactive situation where programmers actually worked at a console and made changes right there on the spot.[7]

By the time the TX-0 was complete in 1957, the Lincoln Lab had already begun work on the much more ambitious TX-1. The TX-1 design never really worked, and very quickly evolved into the TX-2 computer, which was completed in 1958. To get the TX-2 working, they needed to steal some of the core memory, then very expensive, from the TX-0. It seemed at the time that it was not really worth keeping the TX-0 running, so it was loaned, semi-permanently, to the MIT Research Laboratory of Electronics (RLE). Ironically, the TX-2 did not have a long life, with several of its key engineers leaving the project to set up their own company, Digital Equipment Corporation (DEC), in 1959. DEC's first computer, the incredibly influential PDP-1, was a modified version of the robust but now sidelined TX-0.

However, both the more powerful TX-2 and the TX-0, now sitting over in the RLE lab at MIT, had considerable influence on the development of graphical interactive digital computing. Both computers became popular experimental platforms for students working on new forms of computer interaction and graphic development. They would

Ivan Sutherland working with Sketchpad on the MIT TX-2 computer system, 1962.

be the platforms that launched the first work into text editors, code debugging, computer-aided design, speech and handwriting recognition, and artificial intelligence.

Ivan Sutherland – Sketchpad 1962

A young student of Claude Shannon's at MIT submitted his PhD thesis in January 1963.[8] Ivan Edward Sutherland achieved several amazing things in his dissertation research. Working largely alone on the TX-2, mostly between the hours of 3 and 6 a.m., when he could have the computer processors to himself, Sutherland developed what is considered the first fully interactive graphics program, Sketchpad. It is not so much that Sutherland created the first fully interactive computer drawing program, but that in doing so, he also created the first non-procedural programming language and the first object-oriented software system.

Sketchpad was extremely innovative for its time. Not only could you draw figures on the screen, which people had done since Whirlwind, but Sketchpad allowed the user to draw a figure from lines; perform functions on the lines such as scaling, alignment and geometric functions; and then save the lines as an object. Today we think nothing of this procedure. We create words, drawings, 3D models, images, videos and reuse them over and over again. We put them in our documents, in other videos, mash-up images, and bring lots of different digital objects into our presentations. This is normal. But in the early 1960s it was revolutionary, not least as the programming tools to make any of this possible did not even exist yet.

Sutherland not only had to create a drafting system that would store graphical objects, manipulate them and allow them to be reused, modified and combined, but he had to create the programming language, tools and procedures to allow such systems to be built. Years later, when asked by Alan Kay (about whom we will have more to say later) how it was possible to develop all three 'firsts' in just one year – the first fully interactive computer drawing program, the first non-procedural programming language and the first object-oriented software system – Sutherland replied, 'Well, I didn't know it was hard.'

Like his supervisor, Claude Shannon, before him, what Ivan Sutherland did with Sketchpad was not only to create a set of tools which allowed for new possibilities for using computers, and the tools necessary to build these new systems, but to show that it could be done. Working with Sutherland at MIT on the TX-2 were Timothy Johnson and Lawrence Roberts. Using Sutherland's programming techniques, Johnson, in his MS thesis, added 3D solids to Sketchpad, and Roberts added hidden line removal to the 3D solids and the ability to construct new objects from assemblies of 3D solids. One of the most influential outputs of this research was a thirty-minute film made by Sutherland, Roberts and Johnson of Sutherland using Sketchpad which aired on a Boston TV station in 1964.

Ivan Sutherland would go on to design the first heads-up display, and head ARPA from 1964 as it developed the first 'intercomputer connection', what today we know as the Internet. It was Lawrence Roberts, his friend and fellow short-film-maker at MIT, who would head up the actual development of the ARPANET.

From simulation to augmentation

The 1960s quickly developed into a heady time for computer interaction. We tend to think of personal computing and computer interaction as something that arose with the first affordable personal computers in the 1980s, but the foundations of how we interact with our digital devices were foreseen, and largely developed, in the 1960s.

In 1962, an electrical engineer at the Stanford Research Institute (SRI) published a report on his vision of what a concentrated research programme into computer interaction could produce. Doug Engelbart had joined SRI in 1957 and had been working for years on miniaturization of electronics. While serving as a radar technician in the U.S. Navy, on a remote island in the Pacific, he had read Vannevar Bush's 'As We May Think' (1946). Engelbart later said that this was the most significant influence on his thinking and his desire to create systems that would help people think. The purpose of the 1962 report was to convince funders – in this case the government-funded ARPA (Advanced Research Projects Agency) – of the utility of such a project. The report worked and ARPA funded the SRI Augmentation Research Center (ARC).

> By 'augmenting human intellect' we mean increasing the capability of a man to approach a complex problem situation, to gain comprehension to suit his particular needs, and to derive solutions to problems. Increased capability in this respect is taken to mean a mixture of the following: more-rapid comprehension, better comprehension, the possibility of gaining a useful degree of comprehension in a situation that previously was too complex, speedier solutions, better solutions, and the possibility of finding solutions to problems that before seemed insoluble. And by 'complex situations' we include the professional problems of diplomats, executives, social scientists, life scientists, physical scientists, attorneys, designers – whether the problem situation exists for twenty minutes or twenty years. We do not speak of isolated clever tricks that help in particular situations. We refer to a way of life in an integrated domain where hunches, cut-and-try, intangibles, and the human 'feel for a situation' usefully coexist with powerful concepts, streamlined terminology and notation, sophisticated methods, and high-powered electronic aids.[9]

The vision of a new way of working, working with and on computers, was not novel, as we saw with Sutherland's Sketchpad, but it was extremely ambitious in the early 1960s. It was one thing to think that scientists and engineers could use computers interactively to solve problems or design mechanisms, but it was far from apparent then that computers could be used by everyone for everyday tasks. To complicate matters, Engelbart was not just calling for some new tools or systems that would solve specific problems, but for what today we would call a working *environment*: 'We refer to a way of life in an integrated domain . . . [to] the human "feel for a situation" . . . sophisticated methods, and high-powered electronic aids.' This was a manifesto for thinking completely differently about what computers were *for*, and for whom.

The first half of the very lengthy paper outlined Engelbart's principles of learning and working, which he extended to the computer not as a computational device, but as a media machine. He saw the computer, in his then hypothetical system, as 'augmenting' the human intellect. In this way, Engelbart was arguing for the same sort of system as Vannevar Bush. However, Engelbart, unlike Bush, saw his system as not merely enhancing the instruments we use for working and thinking, but transforming, extending and even correcting what constituted working and thinking. What Engelbart was arguing for was similar to what Ivan Sutherland did with Sketchpad, but far more extensive. Where Sutherland had built an interactive drafting program on the computer, but made it do things that could not be done on other mechanisms, thus extending the capabilities of drafting, so Engelbart wanted to create an entire environment that would allow people to do simple, everyday tasks, but extended – augmented – in ways that only digital computers could afford.

More than simply making more effective tools, Engelbart went to great lengths to argue that his proposed system would take full account of how people worked and thought. Though not as explicit as Engelbart, Sutherland too was concerned to augment drafting and modelling in ways that took into account the target user. However, Engelbart was the first person who developed what today we would call a user profile, albeit one that he thought was universal.

The system we want to improve can thus be visualized as a trained human being together with his artifacts, language, and methodology. The explicit new system we contemplate will involve as artifacts computers, and computer-controlled information-storage, information-handling, and information-display devices.

The aspects of the conceptual framework that are discussed here are primarily those relating to the human being's ability to make significant use of such equipment in an integrated system.[10]

The second half of the paper presented, in detail, a hypothetical 'computer based augmentation system'. The description of this system was both radical and unique, and it was filled with features – what Engelbart called 'artifacts' – that today we take for granted, but then were unheard of. The system that Engelbart proposed included a number of ways of working with information on-screen that included 'frames', what we today call windows; documents that were both editable and sharable, very like Google Docs; 'paths' and 'trails' which functioned very similarly to hyperlinks; the ability for users to create processes, as we do today with macros; collaboration tools such as shared comments, annotations and message systems; and the ability to categorize the information and documents on the computer via tags and categories, much as we do with tagging and folders today. The key to the entire system was that it was not intended to support a single individual working alone, but was seen explicitly as a collaborative system for many people working together.

In 1962, however, the only shared computing model available to Engelbart was large centralized processors that a group of people could share via 'terminals'. It is a way of working on computer that is not, in principle, enormously different from our working on the 'cloud', delegating our processing to distant servers that run applications through our browser. My first computing job, in the late 1980s, was running a large research system of terminals connected to a central PDP-11 minicomputer. It was a surprisingly resilient way of working that we continue today, in a very enhanced form, with cloud computing. However, in the 1960s, working on a centralized system meant that the collaborating team had to be more or less in the same place. It was not a truly distributed form of working.

What Engelbart suggested was a way of working on the computer that vastly extended the possibilities of what people thought computers could be used for. He suggested not only a number of new interactive tools, all of which involved new interactive environments bitmapped on a CRT, but a range of interactive devices, including one that he simply called a 'pointer' that could be used by moving it around a flat surface – what would soon become known as a mouse. Engelbart's vision was so advanced that he even saw the limitations of the then immature technologies. He recognized that the resolutions of the existing CRTs were probably far too low for what he was proposing, but he felt that these were limitations that would, in a short time, be overcome, even proposing what acceptable resolutions might be for his hypothetical augmentation system.

Doug Engelbart's 1968 demo

In the report, Engelbart claimed that 'it becomes increasingly clear that there should be action now – the sooner the better – action in a number of research communities and on an aggressive scale.'[11] However, despite extensive and detailed argument, many felt at the time that Engelbart's proposal was both too ambitious for the existing technologies and really rather unnecessary. Did anyone, besides engineers and a few scientists, really want or need to do all this work on computers? Could the computers really cope? Why would universities, institutes and companies give over precious, and expensive, computing time to people working with documents and writing? Who, after all, would be able to afford the expensive systems, or system time, needed to do what effectively was 'secretarial work'?

Despite these misgivings, which seemed extremely compelling at the time, ARPA funded Engelbart's research proposal, and the Stanford Research Institute Augmentation Research Center (ARC) was born. The research and developments undertaken at the ARC over the next six years would astonish the computing establishment and have far-reaching implications that we are still living with today.

The Fall Joint Computer Conference of 1968, held at the Convention Center in San Francisco, presented a number of interesting developments. There were sessions on 'Hand Printed Character Recognition', 'Laboratory Automation', 'Computer Generated Pictures – Perils, Pleasures and Profits' and 'Computer Design Automation'. Doug Engelbart was also there at a panel session, held on 9 December, without papers, entitled 'Human Augmentation through Computers and Teleoperators'. At the session, Engelbart presented the fruits of the ARC's work – the oN-Line System (NLS). Engelbart was seated at a console with a small CRT, which was projected onto a screen via a video. In front of him was a keyboard from a computer terminal, which was familiar to all in the room, but there were also two unfamiliar objects. The one to the left of the keyboard looked like a very small piano keyboard with only five keys, while the one at the right was a small wooden box with three buttons on the top and a cable connecting it to some system under the console. Engelbart welcomed the attendees, saying:

I hope you'll go along with this rather unusual setting and the fact that I remain seated when I get introduced, and the fact that I'm going to come to you mostly through this medium here for the rest of the show, and I should tell you that I'm backed up by quite a staff of people between here and Menlo Park where Stanford Research is located some 30 miles south of here and if everyone of us does our job well, it'll all go very interesting, I think.[12]

Engelbart went on:

The research program that I'm going to describe to you is quickly characterizable by saying, if in your office, you as an intellectual worker were supplied with a computer display, backed up by a computer that was alive for you all day and was instantly responsible, responsive . . . [Laughter] instantly responsive to every action you had, how much value could you derive from that? Well, this basically characterizes what we've been pursuing for many years in what we call the Augmented Human Intellect Research Center at Stanford Research Institute. Now the whole session is going to be devoted to trying to describe and present to you the nature of this program, but unfortunately or fortunately, the products of this program, the technology of it lends itself well to an interesting way to portray it for you, so we're going to try our best to show you rather than tell you about this program.[13]

What Engelbart went on to display was both original and unexpected. As with his 1962 paper, it was not that a lot of people weren't thinking about how to use the computer and to use it as a graphic media interface. However, through the 1960s few had thought of the computer as a personal work device, one that would augment general office work or everyday tasks. The costs involved, and the sheer size of computers, meant, for most people, that this was a specialist technology. However, as Engelbart suggested in his 1962 paper, the computer could be a perfect technology for the everyday and the personal. He was here, in San Francisco, at the end of 1968, to show that it could be done.

The ninety-minute presentation of the NLS far exceeded everyone's expectations. Calmly sitting at his console, Engelbart walked through the many innovations that he and his team at the ARC had developed over the previous six years. These included innovations that are now familiar to us, such as bitmapped screens with overlapping windows, on-screen graphics, hypertext, real-time collaborative editing tools, interactive navigation tools and command line input, a word processor, dynamic file systems and file management systems, revision control and even videoconferencing.

One of the most iconic innovations presented on the day was the small wooden box to Engelbart's right. This was a device invented by Engelbart and his lead engineer, Bill English, to allow a user to move and control a pointer on the screen. Other such devices had been invented before, such as the light-pen from Whirlwind, and there was even a rollerball as early as 1947. However, this small box which moved a pointer by rolling it along a desktop, and using different buttons to cause actions to happen, was our own familiar 'mouse'. Engelbart

Doug Engelbart using the same desk setup as in his 1968 demo. He is using the now familiar mouse and keypad, but also a five-key keyset similar to Baudot's.

and English named it 'the mouse' as the connecting cable came out of the back of the device, rather than the front as contemporary mice do, making it look a bit like the common mouse.

As ubiquitous as the mouse may be today, the most interesting device presented that day, now largely forgotten, was the chorded keyset. The chorded keyset sat to Engelbart's left and was a five-key entry device, very like a piano keyboard, where the operator could enter up to 31 different 'chords' or key-combinations. We have met the chorded keyset before. It is none other than Baudot's keyset. Identical to Baudot's keyset, the five keys corresponded to each of the five bits for each of the letters and special characters of the Latin alphabet. Though the ARC team also added a QWERTY keyboard to the NLS as well, like Baudot's keyset, it was the logical, though not entirely straightforward, interface for entering character messages into a digital device.

Engelbart, like Baudot a hundred years before him, thought that the most logical thing to do when entering characters was to enter the digital codes directly. However, like Baudot's keyset, the ARC chorded keyset never took off, except, interestingly, for Braille users, for, as Donald Murray had realized seventy years before, pushing one letter per character, and characters that the user is already well familiar with, is much easier, and faster, than memorizing digital code. In the long run, though, the mouse–keyboard combination would survive as the dominant input system to today, being only slowly replaced over the past five years or so by touchpads and touch screens.

Interaction with the screen using pointing devices, such as the mouse or the chorded keypad, and the use of interactive graphics, was not revolutionary either. As we discovered with the development of Project Whirlwind at MIT in the late 1940s, the use of a screen to monitor the operation of a computer was almost immediately coupled with an input device, the light-pen. What Engelbart and his team were doing was merely extending uses of the computer as an interactive media device which had already been well developed for CAD from the mid-1950s. In doing so, though, they were extremely innovative and were the first to put all these features together into one system, and to couple the use of the computer with everyday tasks.

In his rather hyperbolic 1994 book, *Insanely Great: The Life and Times of Macintosh, the Computer that Changed Everything*, Steven Levy designated Engelbart's 1968 demo 'the mother of all demos'.[14] Though the demo was exuberantly received at the 1968 conference, and it was, in the long run, highly influential on a small group of engineers that would go on to have a major, albeit indirect, impact on personal computing environments, Engelbart's ARC Lab, and the NLS, would not survive the next few years. The major problems with the NLS were twofold. The first was that the oN-Line System was dependent on a centralized computer that at the time was both expensive and scarce. The 1968 demo was done by networking the console into the mainframe computer thirty miles down the road at the SRI at Menlo Park. Such a configuration was not going to offer much in terms of general applicability.

The second problem was Engelbart himself. In the intervening six years, Engelbart had not only developed the NLS, but also a very complex philosophy of human/computer co-evolution. Drawing heavily on Benjamin Lee Whorf's theory that the sophistication of language controls the sophistication of thought, Engelbart argued, much as many do today, that technology controls how people manipulate information: better technology, better control of information and even collaboration, in which collective IQ would increase immensely. However, his ideas were vastly ahead of his time, if they were even applicable, and many would argue that he was increasingly inflexible in their application.

Though in 1969 Engelbart's lab would successfully open a connection with Leonard Kleinrock's lab at University of California Los Angeles – thus creating the first two nodes of the new ARPANET, the very first Internet, and actively contributing to the development of ARPANET – a major haemorrhage of talent had begun at SRI. This was partly because of new technological developments, which we will talk of next, and partly due to the culture of SRI, which some say had become very confrontational. Doug Engelbart would slip into relative obscurity during the next twenty years, despite his NLS being the first time that all of the elements of what is now the modern personal and mobile computing interface had been assembled in one system. Though Engelbart's NLS demonstrated that such a computing interface could be made, and that it was extremely useful, it was not until computing technology's next major change that such an interface would prove really practical, and ultimately successful.

Computer liberation and the dreams of Ted Nelson

However, Engelbart was not the only person thinking about augmenting humans with computers in the 1960s, and he certainly wasn't the most radical. In 1960, a young graduate student at Harvard started a personal project to create a computer network with a simple user interface, designated Project Xanadu. Theodor (Ted) Holm Nelson was born in 1937, the son of the actress Celeste Holm and her first husband, the later Oscar-nominated director Ralph Nelson. His parents divorced when he was two, and Ted would grow up with his maternal grandparents in Greenwich Village in New York, having little contact with either of his parents. Nelson finished his BA in Sociology at Swarthmore College before going on to a master's at Harvard. While at Harvard, the young Ted Nelson enrolled in a new course on computing for the humanities – yes, they had such courses even in the 1960s. Before beginning the course, Nelson outlined his own vision of what computing should be – personal, literary, mediated and networked.

As his term project for the course, Nelson worked on building a text-handling system where writers could compare, undo and revise their text in a simple way. As he was working on an early mainframe computer, in Assembler (machine code), before anyone had written a fully workable word-processing application, it is not surprising that this extremely ambitious term project was not completed. It did, however, give Nelson the impetus and enthusiasm to press forward with his vision of a user-centric, digital media platform.

Nelson would develop his ideas, and Project Xanadu, further. In 1965 he presented a paper at the Association of Computing Machinery (ACM) conference entitled 'A File Structure for the Complex, the Changing, and the Indeterminate',[15] in which he introduced his concept of hypertext. In his 1974 book, Computer Lib / Dream Machines, Nelson would go on to outline many different categories of hypertext. Though Nelson was the first person to coin the terms hypertext and hypermedia – both introduced in his 1965 article – as well as the word virtuality, his concept of hypertext is different from the one we use today with the World Wide Web. For Nelson, hypertext should not, as no hypertext system existed at the time, simply consist of links to other online documents, but constituted a range of interconnecting and intertextual links, often two-way. In Dream Machines Nelson speaks of hypermaps (as transparent overlays), hypergrams (branching pictures) and branching movies. He outlined environments such as 'stretchtext' with expansive links, and Parallel Textface where two documents can be worked on together on the same screen with full version support. These 'hyperbooks' would consist of

> 'everything' written about the subject, or vaguely relevant to it, tied together by editors (and NOT by 'programmers,' dammit), in which you may read in all the directions you wish to pursue. There can be alternate pathways for people who think different ways.[16]

While Nelson was releasing small insights and glimpses into his greater vision during the 1960s, largely ignored, his 1974 book *Computer Lib / Dream Machines* was a landmark publication. Nelson wrote, edited, formatted and illustrated the book himself, even paying $2,000 for the first print run of 500 copies. It was a large-format, modular publication with Nelson's own hand-drawn illustrations. It was irreverent about almost all claims about computing at the time, and was in two parts. The first part, *Computer Lib*, was about personal computing and its potential to liberate the user. The second part, *Dream Machines*, which was read by flipping the book over and reading from the other side, dealt primarily with the work of Project Xanadu and hypertext, hyper documents and new forms of writing. Though self-published and initially self-distributed, *Computer Lib / Dream Machines* was hugely influential and its first edition would ultimately sell 50,000 copies.

Its radical format and style played well with the rising microcomputer hobbyist culture of the mid-1970s, and harked back to the counter-culture of the 1960s, but it also presented the first manifesto for personal computing. Howard Rheingold, the self-proclaimed critic, writer and teacher of virtual culture, called Nelson's book 'the best-selling underground manifesto of the microcomputer revolution'.[17] Arriving, as it did, just before the release of the first personal computer kit (the Altair 8800 in 1975), *Computer Lib* – for computer liberation – made compelling arguments for the move to personal computing, but as a networked medium.

BRANCHING PRESENTATIONAL SYSTEMS—
HYPERMEDIA

In recent years a very basic change has occurred in presentational systems of all kinds. We may summarize it under the name *branching*, although there are many variants. Essentially, today's systems for presenting pictures, texts and whatnot can bring you different things automatically, depending on what you do. Selection of this type is generally called *branching*. (I have suggested the generic term *hypermedia* for presentational media which perform in this (and other) multidimensional ways.)

A number of branching media exist or are possible.

Branching *movies* or *hyperfilms* (see nearby).

Branching *texts* or *hypertexts* (see nearby).

Branching audio, music, etc.

Branching slide-shows.

Wish we could get into some of that stuff here.

BRANCHING MOVIES

The idea of branching movies is quite exciting. The possibility of it is another thing entirely.

The only system I know of that worked was at the 1967 Montreal World's Fair (Expo 67). At the Czech Pavilion— you will recall that before the crackdown they had quite a yeasty culture going in Czechoslovakia— there were some terrific *kautic* systems going, the use a wall of cubes with slide projectors inside (that rolled toward you and back as they changed their pictures). And then the Movie.

The Czechoslovakian Branching Movie— I forget its real name— had the audience vote on what was to happen next at a number of different junctures. What should she do now, what will he do next, etc. And lo and behold! after they had voted, the lights went down, and that's what would happen next. People agreed that this gave the movie a special immediacy.

I never saw the movie— I waited in line several hours but the line was too long to get into the last showing. So instead I went backstage and talked to Raduz Cincera, who worked out the system. It turns out that it didn't work quite the way people supposed. A lot of people thought that "all the possibilities" had been filmed in advance. Actually, there were always only two possibilities, and no matter *what* the audience had chosen, somehow the film was plotted to come down to the same next choice anyway:

In the actual setup, they simply had two projectors running side by side, with Film A and Film B, and the projectionist would drop an opaque slide in front of whichever wasn't chosen. But Cincera said that audiences almost always chose the same alternatives anyway, so half the movie was hardly ever used...

In the early sixties a movie was making the rounds in which audiences were supposedly allowed to vote on the *ending*— "Mr. Sardonicus." I believe it was called. From the ads it seemed that audiences would be polled as to which last reel to show. Whether the villain was to get his comeuppance, or whatever.

Then there was that Panacolor cartridge projector, mentioned elsewhere, which would have allowed choices by the user

More recently there's the CMX system, also mentioned elsewhere. This is a setup, being jointly marketed by CMX and Memorex, for computer-controlled movie editing. But actually it could also be used as a branching movie system. Essentially the movie itself is stored frame-by-frame (as video) on big disks, made by Memorex; and, under computer control, the output can be switched rapidly among the frames, effectively showing the stored movies. (To my knowledge, the video networks haven't yet recognized the possibilities of this.)

The only trouble is, it's extremely expensive (half a million?), it has an exact storage capacity limited by the number of disk tracks (presumably one track per frame)— perhaps five minutes total one one big unit, but you can buy more— and it can only give its full performance to one viewer at a time.) (Or to be more complete, 1vs.)

It may be that the most practical branching movie system would be a cartridge movie viewer and a big stack of cartridges. When you make your choice, change the cartridge. But of course that's not as much fun as having it happen automatically.

REALITY IS OBSOLETE

The idea that objective reality is perceived by our senses is an obsolete concept. Old truisms like "seeing is believing" become much less believable as we become more aware that, the biological machinery of life itself, transforms images of the physical world before we are made conscious of them. These biological mechanism share many similarities in principle and in application, to other mechanisms observed in the natural environment and those invented for our own use. Since we are becoming more aware of the nature of perception and those mechanisms involved, now is the time to gain control of ourselves and share more discretion in the operation of our own biological machinery. We have entered the age of hyper-reality.

Day-to-day living provides only a limited variety of physical stimulus, and little incentive to manipulate the physiological and psychological processing involved. Man's historical preoccupation with the need to maintain content images of the physical world, is a product of his extreme orientation toward physical survival in a hostile environment. The current evolving society of leisure orientations removes this need for constant images and thereby enhances the opportunities for a more complete use of the sensory apparatus and those related brain functions. Many have turned to drugs or meditation. More specifically it is proposed here, that modern communications technology be employed as a "vehicle of departure" from this need for constant images, to bring about a more complete use of the human technology itself. Hyper-reality is the employment of technology other than the biological machinery, when used to affect the performance of the biological machinery beyond its own limitations. This is almost like making adjustments on a television set, except you are what's plugged in, and the controls are outside your body, being part of whatever technology is interfaced to the body itself. As part of such a man-machine interface you could extend your own mental processes, or if you should choose, you could just diddle with the dials. Hyper-reality is an opportunity to enhance the various qualities of the human experience. Reality is obsolete.

— *Bob Wachspress (see p. DM 8)*
COPYRIGHT 1973 AUDITAC, LTD.

!GREBNETUG

Now, in our time, we are turning Gutenberg around. The technology of movable type created certain structures and practices around the written word. Now the technology of computer screen displays make possible almost any structures and *practices you can imagine* for the written word.

So now what?

For new forms of written communication among people who know each other, jump to "Engelbart" piece, nearby.

To learn about new forms of multidimensional documents for computer screens, jump to "Hypertexts."

Or just feel free to browse.

HYPERTEXT

By "hypertext" I mean non-sequential writing.

Ordinary writing is sequential for two reasons. First, it grew out of speech and speech-making, which have to be sequential; and second, because books are not convenient to read except in a sequence.

But *the structures of ideas are not* sequential. They tie together every whichway. And when we write, we are always trying to tie things together in non-sequential ways (see p. *). The footnote is a break from sequence; but it cannot really be extended (though some, like Will Cuppy, have toyed with the technique).

I have run into perhaps a dozen people who understood this instantly when I talked to them about it. Most people, however, act more bemused, thinking I'm trying to tell them something technical or pointlessly philosophical. It's not pointless at all: the point is, writers do better if they don't have to *write* in sequence (but may create multiple structures, branches and alternatives), and readers do better if they don't have to *read* in sequence, but may establish multiple impressions, jump around, and try different pathways until they find the ones they want to study most closely.

(The astute reader, and anybody who's gotten to this point must be, will have noticed that this book is in "magazine" layout, organized visually by ideas and meanings, for that precise reason. I will be interested to hear whether that has worked.)

And the pity of it is that (like the man in the French play who was surprised to learn that he had been "speaking prose all his life and never known it"), we've been speaking *hypertext* all our lives and never known it.

Now, many writers have *tried* to break away from sequence. I think of Nabokov's *Pale Fire*, of Tristram *Shandy* and an odd novel of Latarre Cortazar called *Hopscotch*, made up of sections ending with numbers telling you where you can branch to. There are many more; and large books generally use many tricks to get around the problem of indexing and reviewing what has and hasn't been said or done already.

However, in my view, a new day is dawning. Computer storage and screen display mean that we no longer *have* to have things in sequence; totally arbitrary structures are possible, and I think that after we've tried them enough people will see how desirable they are.

Page 44 of Ted Nelson's *Dream Machines* from 1974, showing his introduction to 'Hypermedia'.

Project Xanadu failed to materialize despite years of effort by Nelson and others, finally being abandoned in the mid-1990s by its then corporate backer, Autodesk. Project Xanadu exists today as not much more than a few working features and an ageing website (www. xanadu.com). It was a very ambitious project, and, even though little has come of it in the way of working systems, Nelson's ideas were radically influential at the time, and continue to deserve attention today.

Computer Lib / Dream Machines was a book that was handed to every new employee at Apple in the very early days, and its ideas still influence thoughts, right and wrong, about computing culture. In *Computer Lib / Dream Machines* some have seen prefigurations of the World Wide Web, resemblances that Nelson has consistently rejected. He has said that the World Wide Web did fulfil a few of his original proposals, but that the current Internet falls far short of what he envisioned in Project Xanadu. This is certainly true, as Nelson's network was fundamentally based on automatically inter-referencing texts and media objects, and two-way hypertextual links, none of which exists today.

Despite the failed promise of Project Xanadu, what Nelson's book did was to set a clear manifesto for personal computing that had a huge influence on early developments in commercial personal computing. Though I think he would agree that the current state of huge digital corporations dominating vast swathes of the Internet is profoundly contrary to his decentralizing proclamation, 'Down with Cybercrud!', that the technology we use today is profoundly about media and message, rather than mathematics and computation, is in no small part down to Nelson's vision. Nelson was the first, and remains the most radical, advocate for a personal media technology – but a media technology that also radically reimagines what media is and what it is for.

The microprocessor

In contrast, Claude Shannon's information theory, discussed in the last chapter, didn't have much application initially. In fact, for most of the 1950s the notion that you could use Shannon's ideas to improve digital transmission just wasn't generally applicable. With the large, expensive, central processing computers of the day, the processing power needed to perform the algorithms was too expensive. This changed, though, when Russia and the USA got into a space race in the 1960s.

Source coding, what today we would call compression and error correction, became very important in the 1960s. This was because in order to get data back from a craft way out in space, and be able to understand and correctly decode that data, you needed Shannon's information theory. With its first applications on the *Mariner* VI mission in 1969, using source coding algorithms, crisp and clear photos of the surface of Mars were arriving on earth despite millions of miles having been travelled and the immense amount of noise interference. Shannon's theory not only worked, but now had a real application. However, processing power remained a problem and only those with very deep pockets, such as NASA and the military, could afford such immense systems.

In such a world of large, expensive, central processing computers, the contexts for applying Shannon's theories remained small. In 1971, at a source coding workshop held at St Petersburg, Florida, on 'Future Directions', the information theory community reached a consensus. In a famous paper entitled 'Coding is Dead', Robert McEliece said that 'it was time to see this perversion for what it was. Give up this fantasy and take up a useful occupation . . . Coding is dead.'[18] McEliece was not referring to programming (coding) as we mean it today, but to what he saw as the limit of applications for information compression and error correction. The limit to the applications to which this form of information theory worked was, in his mind, and those of many of his colleagues, long since reached.

Information theory was considered a finished endeavour. The limits of what Shannon's theory could do for information transmission on digital devices were – so they all felt at that meeting in Florida in 1971 – known and had been completely worked out and the theoretical field was now obsolete. Robert Gallager, a professor of information theory at MIT at the time, recalled that others suggested to him that he go into a field with more future potential, such as vacuum tubes.[19]

In the discussion at the end of McEliece's paper, a young professor from the University of California San Diego, Irwin Jacob, stood up and said, 'Coding theory is not dead and this is why.' Jacob held up a small piece of plastic no bigger than his thumbnail. It was a very early integrated circuit – a 4-bit integrated shift register, to be precise. Jacob was right. Not only was information theory not dead, but Shannon's ideas were just about to find application at a scale that no one could have ever imagined.

All of our digital devices today use one or more integrated circuits; we call them 'chips'. They are the 'brains' of your laptop, they control your keyboard, they run your mobile phone, your SIM card is an integrated circuit, you even have one on your credit card. The idea is simple. It was invented in 1958 by a young engineer who had just started at Texas Instruments. While working over his holiday break, and having no definitive duties yet, he decided to look into the possibility of an integrated circuit using Ferdinand Braun's once useless semiconductors. Semiconductors had been used to make the transistors for computers since the mid-1950s. Jack Kilby at Texas Instruments thought that he might be able to use the same semiconductors to build the other bits of the computing circuit. Though Kilby built a basic integrated circuit to generate a sine wave on a glass slide using germanium as a semiconductor in 1959, it wasn't until 1970 that anyone managed to build a fully working processor.

Though Texas Instruments is credited with having invented the integrated circuit, Garrett AiResearch, Texas Instruments and Intel all released the first 4-bit microprocessors within months of each other at the end of 1971. Microprocessors would not only change the way that computers worked, but would change what they were used for, how they were used and, most fundamentally, who used them.

Because of the very small size and the low cost of microprocessors, almost overnight Shannon's theory moved from a theoretical concept applied to very expensive and specialist data communications applications, usually from space, to fostering a personal computing revolution. Because Shannon's theory showed how digital information could be moved about without data loss, with microprocessors, this digital data could now be moved within complex integrated systems and between these digital integrated systems. The possibilities became almost endless and, as is the case today, digital processors could be used in any device, for almost any purpose. People started to see the potential almost immediately. You no longer needed to work for a university, for the military or for NASA to build and use a computer. Very soon, anyone could design, build and use a computer. And lots of people did.

Digital media and interactive pedagogy: Xerox PARC and the media machine

As the government contracts were dwindling at Engelbart's Augmented Human Intellect Research Center, a large number of his team, who allegedly were also somewhat disillusioned by Engelbart's alleged autocratic style, moved to the new Xerox PARC. PARC offered researchers the opportunity to do a five-year project pretty much on anything they were interested in, with almost unlimited budgets, so it attracted a large number of young, enthusiastic engineers.

Xerox was, as it is today, a photocopying company, albeit today their devices digitally scan and print. Then, as now, they built, sold and serviced copying and printing machines. However, in the late 1960s Xerox was seeing its market change. As computers increasingly moved into their traditional market, the office, Xerox management felt that they needed a foothold in the new technology. So their chief scientist, Jack Goldman, hired a well-known physicist, George Pake, to set up a second research centre for the company. Pake chose Palo Alto in California, mostly to give the new Xerox researchers some freedom from the company's headquarters 3,000 miles away in Rochester, New York.

Xerox PARC applied a unique model to research. Under their first director, Bob Taylor, a former director at ARPA (Advanced Research

Projects Agency, the funders of the first Internet), PARC would bring
to Palo Alto, as Silicon Valley does today in almost exactly the same
location, the top young computer researchers. As a director of ARPA,
Taylor also knew all the best computer researchers and PhDs in the
U.S. Taylor would attract these leading researchers by not only giving
them almost complete freedom to do whatever research they wanted,
pretty much how they wanted, but providing the funding and facilities
to develop new technologies and an open and collaborative working environment, foreshadowing the open working environments
of today's top Silicon Valley companies. Taylor was not interested in
just any computer research; he wanted Xerox PARC to focus on the
relatively neglected area of computer interaction.

To this end, one of the first hires of the new PARC was Alan Kay, a
young computer engineer from the University of Utah who had worked
there with Ivan Sutherland (the developer of Sketchpad). Just before
joining PARC, Kay had been working with Seymour Papert, who had
developed one of the first simple programming languages designed
to be used by children. Logo Script was inspired by the constructionist
learning theories of Jerome Bruner and Jean Piaget. Their theories
would have a profound impact on Kay's thinking about computers
and the work at PARC, where he was one of the key members of The
Learning Research Group.

The influence of the work of Engelbart and the Stanford Research
Institute was also direct. Not only had many of those working at Xerox
PARC in the early 1970s moved there from SRI, but most of those working in Alan Kay's group, including Kay himself, had been at Engelbart's
'mother of all demos'. However, there were many influences on the
work of the PARC team, of which Engelbart's SRI research was only
one. Alan Kay had been Ivan Sutherland's PhD student at the University
of Utah, but almost everyone in The Learning Research Group had
been involved, in one way or another, in the explosion of research
using computer graphics that had occurred during the 1960s. Research
centres at MIT, Bell Labs, Stanford University, the University of Utah,
the University of Pittsburgh and many other sites had been developing

what was called at the time 'computer graphics' – what today we would call computer-aided design and engineering. From the early work of the Whirlwind team and Ivan Sutherland's Sketchpad, numerous research communities had grown up working on design and simulation of electronics, computer-aided design and manufacturing, speech analysis and simulation, analysis of visual perception and visual interaction, text analysis and so on. However, few were working with computers as personal media devices, in the way envisioned by Engelbart and Nelson, or even as personal devices at all.

Alan Kay's PhD, 'The Reactive Engine' – in which he also introduced his model for KiddiKomp, essentially a laptop computer for children – had been heavily influenced by both Engelbart and Sutherland, and it too had outlined many of the ideas that would find realization at PARC from 1971 to 1975. Starting with the work of the SRI, the vast work of the computer graphics community and constructivist education theories, Kay's team at PARC decided that they needed to move away from the computer as a centralized processor, engaged with by specialist engineers and scientists, to a personal media machine whose primary user would be students, preferably young students. This meant that not only did the nature of the computer have to change, but the way people worked with it had to change too.

From Kay's earlier work with Seymour Papert, and as he had outlined in his PhD, he felt that the real possibility of the microcomputer – the personal computer – would be as an educational device, augmenting not only what we learn, but how we learn.

Imagine having your own self-contained knowledge manipulator in a portable package the size and shape of an ordinary notebook. How would you use it if it had enough power to outrace your senses of sight and hearing, enough capacity to store for later retrieval thousands of page-equivalents of reference materials, poems, letters, recipes, drawings, animations, musical scores, waveforms, dynamic simulations, and anything else you would like to create, remember, and change?[20]

His proposal for PARC was to completely redesign how people, primarily students, worked with computers by building small personal computers and the operating environments. This would involve changing the computer from a large, centralized system, accessed from terminals, to self-contained computers designed for personal use. This would, as they would go on to find out, also involve designing and building a series of other systems that would support these stand-alone, personal computers, such as new printers, networks and video systems, including new, personal, ways of programming.

According to Alan Kay, it was Bill English, the co-inventor of the mouse, who helped him set up the team for, as Kay said, 'I had always been a lone wolf and had no idea how to do it.'[21] Kay realized that he needed a group of people who had the temperament to finish projects, rather than just start them.

Learning Research Group (LRG) [was] to be as vague as possible about our charter. I only hired people that got stars in their eyes when they heard about the notebook computer idea. I didn't like meetings: didn't believe brainstorming could substitute for cool sustained thought. When anyone asked me what to do, and I didn't have a strong idea, I would point at the notebook model and say, 'Advance that.'[22]

At the beginning, Kay and his team worked with colleagues and university students to work out how to develop the operating environments for personal learning. There was already a precedent for this running out of the University of Illinois, which Kay and his team had visited in 1972. The PLATO system (Programmed Logic for Automatic Teaching Operations) had been developed by a laboratory assistant, Donald Bitzer, on the recommendation of his boss, the physicist Daniel Alpert and the dean of engineering at Illinois, William Everett, in the early 1960s. The project actually began in 1959, but the first system, PLATO I, was launched in 1960. The goal of PLATO was to provide an interactive, graphical and textual teaching and learning

system, and it was used by a number of universities with great success up to the 1980s. I remember being a willing guinea pig for a new
course using PLATO IV at Illinois State University in 1976, and being
amazed by its rich (albeit monochrome) graphics and its pedagogical
sophistication.

The PLATO that Kay and his team saw in 1972 was also PLATO IV,
which had just been released that year. Offering the lecturer not only
a rich computer graphic environment, with many features to simulate
and graph complex interactions; graphics tools for drawing sophisticated and often animated diagrams; speech and music synthesizers,
even music notation editors; interaction with keyboards, mice and
light-pens; and support systems for assessment, PLATO was the state
of the art in educational software for the time, and remains more
advanced than many contemporary online learning systems today,
both technically and theoretically.

However, in Kay's mind, PLATO remained flawed, first because it
remained, at that time, a centralized processing system using terminals,
but mostly because he saw it as simply reproducing existing educational
practice. Being a student of Papert, Kay felt that there was more potential in experimenting with how this new digital medium could transform education, rather than simply mimicking and extending it. Soon
after seeing PLATO, Kay decided that working with adults was too
limiting.

As early as the summer of 1971, Kay worked to refine his KiddiKomp
idea into a more workable design. His first version, the miniCOM, was
simple with a bitmapped display, a pointing device and some storage. Also included was a new programming language that Kay called
'Smalltalk'. Kay said that he called it Smalltalk as a reaction to what
he saw as the

'IndoEuropean god theory' where systems were named Zeus, Odin,
and Thor, and hardly did anything. I figured that 'Smalltalk' was so
innocuous a label that if it ever did anything nice people would be
pleasantly surprised. 'Smalltalk' was meant to invoke something

simple, but also useful: 'Smalltalk' – as in 'programming should be a matter of . . .' and 'children should program in . . .'[23]

This initial 'egg', as Kay called his big ideas, would develop at Xerox PARC into an innovative programme of experimentation with children and teenagers on what the LRG called 'Personal Dynamic Media'.[24] Over this period, the LRG and their young assistants developed the devices that we see as being foundational to personal computing today. The environments that PARC's LRG developed in the early 1970s included a full Graphical User Interface (GUI) with Windows, Icons, Menus and Pointers (WIMP) that we are familiar with today. PARC also developed working models for the personal computer and design prototypes for the laptop and the tablet. Their systems included laser printers and local area networks (LANs). They also included bitmapped screens and rich text fonts, offering a means of encoding an almost limitless diversity of information and media.

Key to these developments was a return to the idea of the digital as a medium and as a message. Influenced by the work of Marshall McLuhan, the LRG sought to develop media environments with

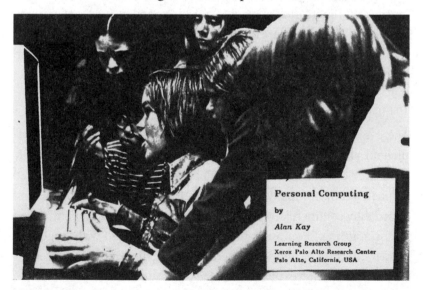

Children working on the early Alto computer at Xerox PARC lab, 1974.

'"Devices" which variously store, retrieve, or manipulate information in the form of messages embedded in a medium'.

> Every message is, in one sense or another, a simulation of some idea. It may be representational or abstract. The essence of a medium is very much dependent on the way messages are embedded, changed, and viewed. Although digital computers were originally designed to do arithmetic computation, the ability to simulate the details of any descriptive model means that the computer, viewed as a medium itself, can be all other media if the embedding and viewing methods are sufficiently well provided. Moreover, this new 'metamedium' is active – it can respond to queries and experiments – so that the messages may involve the learner in a two-way conversation. This property has never been available before except through the medium of an individual teacher. We think the implications are vast and compelling.[25]

With an emphasis on this new, dynamic metamedium, the LRG played a large role in the turn of emphasis in computing from engineering towards the creation of whole new objects and new ways of working with them. The very nature of the digital computer as a medium in itself was realized at Xerox PARC in those years – to a degree.

The rise of corporate personal computing

There is an apocryphal story about how a young Silicon Valley entrepreneur visited the LRG at Xerox PARC in 1979 and was completely captivated by what he saw. So much so that he immediately returned to his fledgling company, Apple, to start what would become the first affordable, commercially available personal computer that embodied the principles of computer interaction which began with Engelbart at SRI and were developed at Xerox PARC. This young entrepreneur was, of course, Steve Jobs, one of the two founders of Apple, and the personal computer would be the Macintosh. The accepted history goes on to assert that because of Xerox's narrow and blinkered focus on copiers, and the then current technologies, they missed the opportunity that Apple, IBM and others capitalized on.[26]

Like all apocryphal stories, it is in part true, but mostly overstated. As is often the case, there was no *aha!* moment, but as Silicon Valley is a relatively small place with lots of people moving between companies, much was already known about the work of the LRG at Xerox PARC by Apple staff long before Steve Jobs's visit. Jobs was visiting, actually, because one of his project managers, Jef Raskin, who wanted to do a lot more with the Apple II's user interface, had been pushing Jobs into visiting the PARC for a while. However, what ultimately became the Macintosh was very different from what was happening on Xerox's Star microcomputer.

The Apple Lisa had even more in common with what the PARC were doing, and even more sympathy with the work of Ted Nelson, than the Macintosh did, but Jobs pushed the Macintosh over the Lisa – falling out with his co-founder, Steve ('Woz') Wozniak, in the process – feeling that it could compete better with the first PCs that were being produced by IBM and others at the time. It is interesting that, in the end, the developments at Apple, IBM and Microsoft owed more to Engelbart and even Nelson than they did to the PARC developments, reproducing, even simulating, office and lab work over education.

The history of the development of the personal computer, the World Wide Web and mobile technologies is beyond the scope of this book. Though that too is a fascinating story, it has been told in many other places and it is, from our point of view here, not a story that adds much to our understanding of digitality. It is not that by the early 1980s everything we have today was understood, invented or at least prototyped. Nothing could be further from the truth. Nor should we assume that the paths that these technologies took, and their uses in society, were already fixed. However, what constitutes the digital today – digitality, what it is, how it works, what it is primarily for – was well established by the mid-1980s.

The content of the computer is descriptions of processes; the ability of computers to simulate the details of any descriptive model means that the computer, viewed as a medium itself, can be all other media if the embedding and viewing methods are sufficiently well provided.[27]

The consequences of going digital were similar in personal computing at the end of the twentieth century to what they were in telecommunications at the beginning of the century. There was an explosion of information and, hence, in its production, exchange and storage, but mostly in how it was used. As the codes used for digital data already worked with the existing tape punch and card punch input mechanisms, as well as existing teleprinters, from the 1950s onwards information could be entered, stored, processed and retrieved in large quantities – as digital codes. With the almost simultaneous development of the graphical user interface (GUI) and bitmapped graphics, computers never again had very much to do with computation. They were now document and data emulators and processors, repository managers and media stores. From the early 1960s the computer was destined, irreversibly, to become a media and information collecting and processing machine, albeit one that worked with media in a completely novel way.

What I have tried to show in this chapter is that the vast diversity, and hence scale, of the digital objects that we today create, store, share and transform, as well as the many environments on which we work digitally, are not the simple result of a sequence of technological innovations, but are the consequence of the transformation of the computer in the 1950s, '60s and '70s from an electronic calculator to a digital media processing machine. The coupling of digital encoding with electronic processing implied the vast multiplication of objects, uses and applications, the vast digital archive we have today. It also implied, though this was never assured, that these electronic logic machines would be primarily used for creating, storing, modifying, sharing, transforming and multiplying media objects – documents, images, video, messages, sounds and so on – for use by people in their everyday lives. The enormous expansion of technology over the past twenty years, as well as the massive expansion in data capacity and processing power, are not the cause of the information explosion, but the consequence of 'going digital'. The Information Age was the result of digital encoding and its consequences, as was understood back in the 1960s and '70s by Engelbart, Kay, Nelson, the PLATO team, Apple and a host of others. The primary consequence of digitality is not computation, but messages and media.

5

MEDIA CLONES, MULTIPLE RENDERINGS: THE CONSEQUENCES OF THE DIGITAL

Today we live in a world of ubiquitous digital media. Digital information, digital media and digital devices are everywhere. Sixty years ago, there were but a few hundred digital computers in the entire world. These were mostly in laboratories or part of very large military installations. Each was the size of a small house, or larger, requiring dozens of technicians and engineers to keep it running. In terms of processing power and storage, despite their enormous size, the power of these devices was minuscule compared to what we all carry around in our pockets today. However, despite their adolescence – having only been around for a few years – and their rarity and largely specialized roles, before digital computers were 25 years old most of the components, qualities and environments we find familiar today existed in some form. This was in part because, though there were but a few digital computers back then, there were literally thousands of digital devices in the world – devices that had been around, and digital, for almost a hundred years. This book has traced some of the various and often disconnected histories that began with the digital telegraph and went on to shape our current digital world.

The digital world we live in today still contains the traces of these histories. The digital codes for the letters I am now typing are not only based on the principles of Baudot, but retain many of the same codes, largely for the upper-case Latin letters, as the Baudot–Murray code. Embedded in every sentence we type, on any of our devices – if we are using capital Latin letters – are the traces of the very origins of digitality.

The computer chips that are the processing hearts of our digital devices work along the same principles as Claude Shannon's relays that he observed at MIT in the mid-1930s. Our devices feed information into the processor as digital codes following, mostly, the principles of Turing's Universal Machine outlined in 1936. They can do the vast amount of work needed to process digital information at high speed, without error, because of Shannon's information laws that he presented in 1948. Despite the limitations of Turing's conceptual machine, our computer chips process vast quantities of information because they work in parallel, just like Whirlwind did at the end of the 1940s. Even the principles of magnetic, or now transistor (flash), memory storage were in use by the late 1940s.

We also access all of our digital devices – whether on our phone, our laptop or our toaster – via a graphical user interface (GUI). As we saw in the last chapter, the fundamental principles of the GUI, even of the Web, existed by 1973. With the rise of the microchip, and the personal computer in the 1970s, the potentials of distributed digital devices, rather than large central processors, seemed obvious to the Xerox PARC team, and to the new start-up companies of Silicon Valley. However, it wasn't until 1984, with the Apple Mac, that our way of engaging with the personal computer became widely available, with a fully implemented 'window, icon, menu, pointer' (WIMP) interface, as well as the WYSIWYG ('what you see is what you get') media editing and viewing. Even the interrelating of digital devices that we take for granted today existed by the mid-1970s, being largely based on the callow technologies of the digital telegraph. Personal computers with display screens, mice and keyboards; printers that printed what we saw on the screen; wired – though not Wi-Fi – networks; digital images and video, with videoconferencing; spreadsheets; word processors; imaged editors; 2D and 3D design systems; even games; all were pervasive, in one form or another, by the late 1970s.

Some things were not immediately anticipated. Though smartwatches are still trying to catch up with Dick Tracy, almost everyone working on computers and computer interaction before 1970 failed to anticipate miniaturization, which nonetheless moved quickly from the early 1970s onwards. Though storage has grown exponentially, and shrunk exponentially in price, since the end of the 1970s, few anticipated the consequences of extraordinarily large amounts of information and processing power. Despite this, pretty much all the constituents of our contemporary digital world were in place before Steve Jobs even dreamed of the Apple Mac – with one exception.

You would think that as digitality arose from telecommunications its application to the telephone would have been obvious from an early date. However, this was not the case. There is the famous prediction by Nikola Tesla, of radio fame, given in an interview in 1926, that the world could be covered by a wireless power system that would provide energy and information.

> When wireless is perfectly applied the whole earth will be converted into a huge brain, which in fact it is, all things being particles of a real and rhythmic whole. We shall be able to communicate with one another instantly, irrespective of distance. Not only this, but through television and telephony we shall see and hear one another as perfectly as though we were face to face, despite intervening distances of thousands of miles; and the instruments through which we shall be able to do this will be amazingly simple compared with our present telephone. A man will be able to carry one in his vest pocket.[1]

However, Tesla was not referring to extending the then digital telegraph to telephony, or even television. His vision was a purely analogue one. He was predicting the extension of radio signals, purely analogue at the time, to carry voice, image and information. Though our current mobile communications, and our Wi-Fi, use radio signals to transmit and receive, as Tesla predicted, they carry not analogue information, but digital information. However, at least for our mobile telephones, this was not always the case.

Mobile phones have been around for some time, the first being developed not long after Tesla's prediction in the 1930s. Mobile radio telephones were used in the Second World War, with RCC (Radio Common Carrier) phones available for public use from the 1960s. The first cellular networks (1G) were available in Tokyo from 1979, and in parts of Scandinavia from 1981. However, though all these telephones were *mobile*, they all used analogue radio signals to transmit voice. The first digital mobile telephone networks (2G) were not available until the early 1990s. Like digital television and radio, digital mobile telephony was part of an ongoing development of a successful and existing technology.

Interestingly, during the Second World War, Bell Labs was tasked with developing the X-System, the encrypted radiotelephone link between Washington and London. As it was very difficult, if not impossible, to fully encrypt analogue voice signals, Bell Labs developed a method of 'quantization', sampling the analogue voice signal into digital bits which could easily, and completely, be encrypted. What was essentially a digital voice transmission system, like our cellnets today, saw little use outside of military applications after the war.

Wi-Fi, on the other hand – the brand name for wireless local area networks coined by the Interbrand Corporation in 1999 – was the outcome of a seemingly unimportant decision by the U.S. Federal Communications Commission (FCC) in 1985. One of the FCC's engineers, Michael Marcus, suggested that they take several of the 'garbage bands' (frequencies mostly used by microwave ovens) out of licence and open them up for new communications applications. However, it wasn't until 1991, when NRC Corporation wanted to use the frequencies to connect their new cash registers, that they began the work on a standardized format for the now overcrowded 900 MHz, 2.4 GHz and 5.8 GHz bands. The now familiar IEEE 802.11a and 802.11b standards were not ratified until December 1999 and January 2000 respectively, but this work to standardize broadcast over these now unlicensed frequencies opened up the immediate potential for the current Wi-Fi networks which became pervasive internationally within five years.

Anticipated or not, inevitable or not, designed or not, we have the digital culture we have today. It was not determined, it could have been otherwise, but it emerged, sometimes cobbled together. It continues to hold shadows of other media, and of earlier digital technologies, but is constantly incorporating, and converging with, other forms of media and other technologies. It has moved from a telecommunications medium in a world of diverse media and manifold information technologies, to mediate all other media – to become *the* media and information technology. It has done this by incorporating the qualities of other media, but also by extending them, augmenting them, to extraordinary scales. However, it also does some things that no other medium does, or has ever done, by delegating rendition to an algorithmic process.

Persistent, multiple and mobile: a medium like all others

So what is it that binds this ill-assorted collection of bits together and keeps the kludge going? What exactly is the digital? What is digitality? As I suggested at the beginning, and have tried to show throughout, what makes the digital *digital* is not 1s and 0s, or even *ons* and *offs*, but *encoding*. Baudot's idea was simple: take the most basic form of information – presence and absence, hole or no hole, on or off – and use this to encode letters. Five-bits were all that was needed, then. What he did not anticipate, what Shannon realized seventy years later, was that this ordinary idea of using the most simple form of information as a code would allow us to encode almost all other information, no matter how complicated, no matter how far away, no matter in what media. Without the code, binary is just a light switch.

The digital is the code, but codes have to be processed to make any sense. So to separate the code, and the encoding, from its processing would be impossible. What the processing – the algorithms, the operating systems, the network protocols, the apps – does is to render the encoding. This *rendering* is what makes an encoding, unreadable and unusable, into a readable, usable, interactive medium. The key here is that digital encoding is in no way a representation. It is an encoding that presumes a conventional outcome, a set of instructions, which will translate this encoding into some preordained media performance, or some transformation leading to a media performance. But this rendition, the ensuing media performance, has no necessary coupling with the code – except by convention. The rendition of code, the performance, can be processed, by other code, in any way, as long as it is algorithmic (a sequence of logical steps), and within the capabilities of the technology.

There are a number of qualities or features which distinguish something as a medium, or at least as a communicative mass medium. Primarily these are persistence, reproducibility and mobility. All media technologies, from the earliest writing on clay tablets and stone, to twentieth-century media technologies such as printing, phonograph, radio and television, have these qualities. It is true that, in some instances, such as early television, qualities such as persistence did not yet exist, beyond the transmission, yet they could have but for certain economic limitations. They were also added to the media very soon afterwards.

Persistence is the quality whereby a medium acts as a carrier of the message that endures over time. We can say that our voice, spoken in the air or on the original analogue telephone, is communication, but it does not persist or endure, at least not for very long. Our words are lost almost as soon as they are spoken, never to be heard again. We may now be used to pervasive predictions of the loss of our information and memories by 'fragile' digital media, the most recent coming from Google's vice-president Vint Cerf, who recently warned that our digital data could be wiped out by tech upgrades.[2] However, for twentieth-century historians the real memory black hole came with the pervasive use of the telephone from the 1920s until the advent of general public email in the 1980s. Unlike before, when people used to send each other letters, telegrams and even just short notes, during this period many people just made a telephone call, thus denying any persistence to the conversation. In this period, much of history might as well have been prehistory.

Mass media must have a means of keeping the message so that it can be saved, in a stable form, stored and used over and over again.

Persistence was one of the key qualities of the creation of writing. Words could be inscribed with symbols on some medium and be kept, enduring in time, for future reference or reading. Jacques Derrida, the French philosopher and semiotician, famously stated that 'The sign is born, at the same time as imagination and memory, at the moment when it is demanded by the absence of the object for present perception.'[3] Media too are born at this moment when our words and works, our memories, must persist.

Another key quality of media is that they can be copied – reproduced. This may be, as it was for most of history, a laborious process of copying by hand, but such copying, and even translation of works, is what allowed medieval Europe to read the scientific, philosophical and mathematical works of the more advanced Islamic scholars, as well as the works of the long-past Greeks and Romans that the Islamic world had preserved through copying and translation. Copying is a form of preservation, of persistence, but also allows for the 'mass' in mass media. This multiplication of media objects, as one of its essential qualities, allows for the objects to exist in many places at the same time. The greatest advantage of printing, phonographic recording, photography and film, which lends them their primary purpose, is that all these media technologies are based on copying – making many exact duplicates of the original, which can exist in many places at the same time, even many different places at many different times. In fact, all of these technologies are predicated on copying. None of them makes much sense as a mass medium unless they can be copied – can be made multiple.

Television, at least pre-video, and radio seem to be exceptions here. Neither requires copying, per se, as both are broadcast media. However, this is not exactly true in that, in a very real sense, television and radio are all about copies. Being not only the first electronic media, but also the first broadcast media, television and radio broadcasts were multiplied, on a vast scale, via electronic signals received by thousands and, ultimately, millions. Like our Internet and Wi-Fi today – both based on similar modulated signals – television and radio were copied and multiplied by signal transmission and reception rather than by imprint. However, until recently these were analogue signals rather than modulated digital signals. This model of distributing media works – making them multiple via signals – has now become *the* model for the Internet and the cloud.

Of course, it should be remembered that television and radio were also distributed as imprints. With the rise of syndication based on recordings being distributed for broadcast throughout countries and even the world, as soon as it was economically and technically feasible both television and radio were copied – imprinted onto tapes or vinyl discs to be replayed at some point distant in time and space.

The major reason for media to be reproducible, as all mass media are primarily industries, is to be able to sell copies, or the advertising that goes with distributing to millions or even billions of viewers. This leads us to the next, and perhaps most important, quality of media – their mobility.

Mobility, in a stable form, is essential to mass media. If media were not imprints, or signals, that were in a stable form, and could not also *travel* without significant change, then they could not be *mass* media. Mass media depend, by definition, on being able to be employed by a mass of people, individually or in groups, at the same time and in many different and distant places. Bruno Latour, a French philosopher and historian of science, has associated these 'immutable mobiles', as he calls them, with the rise of modern science and modernity itself. Only when there were the media technologies, and genres of demonstration, that could provide stable (immutable), persistent, multiple and mobile accounts of experimentation and scientific discovery could science be shared and developed in cooperation (more or less).[4]

Mobility characterizes all forms of media, especially mass media. The printing press, developed from the fifteenth century, not only saved on the laborious process of copying books, but served primarily to allow exact copies to be produced cheaply enough, and in large enough numbers, to travel throughout the world, to places and people who did not before have access to text. This would transform literacy around the world – over time. The rise of mechanical and electronic media in the nineteenth and twentieth centuries would extend and augment this process. Not only did publishing and distribution of printed texts boom in the nineteenth century, but so did, as we all know, the media technologies of photography, sound recording and film. These technologies would produce astounding numbers of works and multitudes of copies of photographs, records, tapes and films. These copies, which were stable (more or less), would travel the globe, always as copies. It was in the twentieth century that we got the first signal-based, electronic media – radio and television. Though less stable, or persistent, initially, these media would travel further and wider than any other.

A medium is a material on which an imprint is made so it can persist, be copied and travel. This is as true for film as it is for the printed word, as true for the phonograph as it is for the photograph. When Claude Shannon started to think about television signals in the 1940s, and how they could be compressed and made more efficient, he recognized that the medium of television, and radio, was not the microphones, the cameras or even the radio and television sets, but the signal. Often treated as an amalgam, an assemblage, of cameras, writers, lights, mixers, actors, recording systems, producers, broadcast systems, antennas, TV sets and viewers, what distinguishes television and radio from earlier media is that they exist as a *signal*. This is also what connects them with the digital. Like all media, television, radio and the digital are technically mediated and, therefore, translated into a new form, but these twentieth-century signal-based media are not imprinted onto some surface, but translated into an electrical signal. This *translation* into an electrical signal not only caused problems, the ones that Shannon sought to solve in his 'Information' paper of 1948, but created whole new possibilities.

It has been said that without Shannon there would have been no Internet. Now, backwards history is always a dangerous endeavour, but Shannon's redefinition of information as predictability in a signal, and his demonstration that the most lossless signal was a digital one, certainly was seminal to most of the developments in digital technology even today. However, while his association of information, predictability (entropy) and signals was equally applicable to analogue signals, and transformed analogue signal transmission in the 1950s and '60s, it was his recognition that the digital was the most efficient encoding that created a critical distinction between digital and analogue media.

The digital is similar to television and radio as a medium, and has more in common with these than it does with the printed word, photography, phonographs and films, even though television and radio were some of the last media to be become digital. It is similar in that the digital signal is, in the end, just a modulated analogue signal, albeit a very structured one. Whether over a wire, or optical fibre or through the air (via Wi-Fi), digital signals are basically analogue signals, transmitted through these *channels* in the same way as were television and radio signals, or the signals for telephones and telegraphs. At the most basic level of the signal, the digital is as messy as are all communication signals.

What Baudot had hit upon, back in the 1870s, was that the best way to transmit a signal, with the minimum amount of loss, was to encode it in digital codes. Almost another eighty years passed before Shannon explained why it was that digital encoding offered the least loss of information in a message signal when mediated mechanically, by electronics. For mass media then – and largely still now – getting the message through is not much of a problem. It had already been successfully solved in Baudot's day. The phonograph had just been invented, photography had been around for more than thirty years and film was not far away. In thirty years, there would be radio, which raised this method of a single message distribution to many listeners to a new level, and television was not far behind. As with print, what you needed was a stable medium that could be mass-produced, or mass-broadcast. Baudot's breakthrough was, however, to recognize that if you needed to send not just a single message to many people, but countless numbers of messages to countless numbers of people, then you needed another approach.

In this sense, the most popular media today, social media and messaging, are simply augmentations of the telegraph. The early Internet bulletin boards, messaging, email and SMS are basically forms of telegraph and telex. What we do when we send an SMS or post to a social media site is essentially to send a text message from us to one other person, or a small number of friends. This is what a telegraph did. All other media were messages sent from one 'sender' to multiple, often vast numbers of, 'receivers'. Today we have more elaborate augmentations of the telegraph: Facebook, Twitter, Weibo, VKontakte, Pinterest, Instagram, Telegraph, Qzone, WhatsApp and so on. However, they all operate on the same basic principle as Baudot's telegraph, sending a single message, digitally, to one or a few recipients.

The digital, as a medium, is capable of more than this. What makes digitality different is that, unlike even television, the digital mediates the object by both encoding it and then processing it every time it is presented. Television, like radio, is not an encoding, strictly speaking. It does translate the image, and sound, into a signal, but that signal simply modulates a similar device at the receiving end, conceptually not very different from the Hughes telegraph. When a broadcaster speaks into a microphone in a radio studio, the sound of their voice causes vibrations that the microphone renders into an electrical signal. This signal is transmitted and received by a radio, somewhere, and an identical electrical signal is rendered back into sound via a speaker which is a kind of reverse microphone. This signal may be modulated to improve it, or amplify it, but it cannot be changed into anything else but noise. Television, analogue television that is, does the same with light, translating it into an electrical signal that is translated back into light in the television set. Vladimir Zworykin's kinescope was basically a reverse iconoscope. Digital media, from Baudot to today, do something very different: they process the message into a code. Like other electronic media, digital does then transmit this code as a signal, but at the other end there is no fixed rendering, there is no reverse digitizer. Of course there was, in Baudot's day, but this was because Baudot saw the encoding only serving telegraphs. By the

1950s, with the development of digital computers, there was no fixed rendering of digitally encoded information at the receiving end. There was no fixed rendering of the digital information at any point – there was nothing but *reformation*. The digital we see and work with on our screens or devices is not a rendering, but an ongoing production – an algorithmic achievement.

So how does this achievement actually work in the digital? Let's say that you just captured an image with your phone. Perhaps you were on holiday and were taking snaps of your family on the beach, or you were just taking an image of something on the way home from work. It doesn't really matter. First of all, from the moment that you pressed the button on your phone, to the instant later that you see the image on your screen, your image has gone through a minimum of ten copies. Of course, the number of copies depends on what phone you have, how it processes the image, what settings you have, the light conditions, and many other factors, and this is the point. You can be sure that just the process of taking an image has created a plethora of copies – a plethora of variable renderings.

Now let's say that you are now sitting with a cup of something warm at a café and you want to review your images from the day. You open up the images on your screen, usually seeing a number at the same time, seeing just the 'thumbnails'. More copies. Your device, whether a phone, tablet, laptop or whatever, has had to go to the hard drive, or flash memory, and copy a number of blocks into the working memory, the RAM. It has then copied various bits of this digital code from the RAM to the processors, of course only after copying up a number of bits of other code to tell it how to process the encoded image. Each process copies bits of your images from one place to another: from memory, to the bus, to the processor, to the bus, to the screen driver, to the screen. A legion of copies are running around your device constantly, constantly being checked, recopied, processed, copied again and again. All of this copying assumes that you are only working on your local device. Perhaps you don't have access to Wi-Fi or 3G. Once you are connected to the Internet, or simply connected via wire or Bluetooth to other devices, the multiplicity of your digital image increases enormously.

Unlike analogue media, which certainly depend on copies, digital media do not depend on copies only for distribution, but for their very existence. If, in the story above, you took your images with a film camera, rather than a digital camera, you would also be creating copies, though far, far fewer. However, each of your film image copies is just one move, one copy, from one stable media impression to another stable media impression, each impression being a duplicate of the previous one. The new, or the old, copy of your film image doesn't need to reproduce itself each time it is viewed, moved, picked up, put in a box, mailed to someone and so on. Each recreation of your digital image, each time you wish to view it, move it, store it, send it, involves a multitude of copies. The digital is multiplicitous by necessity. Without the ability to multiply itself, the digital object exists only as encoding.

Never the same: digital objects as performance

We might think that as the medium of television and radio is the signal, digital is but a signal multiplied. Though it does rely on the transmission of signals, either locally in the device or widely over networks, the digital is not really a broadcast medium multiplied. As Baudot realized with his telegraphs, the power of the digital is needed not when you have to transmit one message to many, but when you have to transmit many messages to many. It is not surprising that digitality arose with the telegraph, a medium of one to one, on a vast scale. Nor is it surprising that our current network infrastructure arose with the telephone, a similar one-to-one media. However, unlike the analogue telephone, the medium of the digital, which is also persistent and multiplicitous, is the encoding and the processing of this code.

Because the medium of digitality is the encoding and its processing – digital data and the programs that process it – digital media are this dynamic, complex, diverse, socio-technical entanglement of digitally encoded data, code, apps, chips, display devices, keyboards, mice, trackpads, touch screens, storage devices, operating systems, networks, cables, electronics, desktops, images, sounds and text that we all produce, co-produce, engage with, use and view. It is a habitat that we all live in, work in, play in. A habitat that effects and affects us, and we effect it – it demands interaction. Of course, this could be said of any media. Some of the technological and human agents that I listed above, which are but a fraction of the digital list, would be different, but any media could be defined by a changing assemblage of technologies and people. However, each medium has some medium that binds it, that gives it some coherence.

For digital media this is the necessary integration of digital encoding and its processing by algorithmic programs. This integration, amalgam, of encoding and processing has existed since Baudot's first telegraph, as it did up to the last telex machine, although the algorithmic processing was mechanical rather than programmatic. After Shannon had shown that relays could do logic, and Turing showed how you could make a machine that could do algorithms, machines were built that could solve problems algorithmically. These first electronic computers would solve problems by following instructions. However, like the analogue machines before them, they followed a set of instructions hardwired into the machine, or at least wired with changeable plugboards of wires. It was quickly realized that the machine, as Alan Turing has suggested, could be better used if the instructions could themselves be encoded as the data was, for Claude Shannon had shown by then that the most efficient encoding was indeed digital encoding. So, by the 1950s, the medium was integrated. Encoding of information, letters, numbers, pixels on a screen, data points and the instructions for their fashioning could all be designated by a digital encoding.

Digitally encoding everything – the data, the instructions, the storage, the processing, the display – changed digital from a messaging system to a medium. More importantly, it became a performative medium. From the very early days of Whirlwind, one of the very first fully digital electronic computers, what the computer did, its actual functioning, was performed on a screen, not internally, as is true of all mechanisms, but publicly, as a spectacle. The ultimate purpose of Baudot's digital telegraph was also to *perform* the message publicly, as there is not much point in sending a telegram that no one reads. However, when digital encoding was coupled with processing, as was needed to have something like a digital electronic computer, then this performativity became new, very much more versatile and extraordinary.

All media are performative, but digital media are different. When you perform a film, a book or even a television show, the viewer – the user, if you will – is not intended to interact directly with the performance. Of course, we all do interact with these media in different ways, and there is a great deal of media studies devoted to how the *audience* interacts with what is allegedly a non-interactive media. We also know from the past fifty years of literary theory that the most important person for the meaning of a text is not the writer, but the reader. However, this kind of interaction is not what I am referring to. From the first days of digital computers, from the first work on the Whirlwind computer, a fundamental quality of digital media has been that it is interactive in the sense that we, the users, are culpable in the outcome of what we see and hear. We are not just implicated in what we think about the performance, we directly influence the performance. We do have applications that work pretty much like a television set or a book, or even like a phonograph. There have even been some applications written that mimic these earlier media in extraordinary detail. When we play a movie from a DVD, the experience is designed to be very like what we would experience in the cinema, only smaller. However, these applications are *designed* to be *not like* digital media, but use digital media to be *like* older, analogue media. The difference here is that, rather than performing the film media, in a digital format the performance has to be designed. Even if there is little or no interaction from the user, the interaction, the action of designing its performance, is not part of the digital object. It is something done to the digital object, and this something can be done differently, by any number of different people, at any stage of its performance.

This points to the final quality of digital media, that is different from all other media: that every performance of a digital object is different. Analogue media, which are copied a few, or even many, times are performed in homogeneous ways. Each and every copy plays pretty much the same way as all the others. Now, as any hi-fi enthusiast will tell you, the performance of a phonograph record will vary enormously dependent on the configuration, and the quality, of the hi-fi equipment.[5] We also all know that there is a vast difference between the impact of a film viewed in a cinema, especially if it has a large screen, and when we see it on an aeroplane. There is also a difference between the play of a game on our game centre with a large screen and on our mobile phone. However, the performativity of digital media happens at a much deeper level, at the level of the code and processes. Though the performative equipment has a crucial impact on the performance of any media, especially affectively, the equipment that plays analogue media can only enhance, or diminish, the quality and impact of the imprint. It cannot do anything much with the imprint itself except modulate it through electronics or lenses. Digital media are different. Though the performative instruments certainly affect the quality and impact of the performance, there is no imprint.

Let's consider the image you took with your phone that we discussed above. Not only is it creating a small army of copies every time you do something, anything, with your image, each and every copy of the digital code that is that image is not being reproduced, or even rendered, as an analogue medium does; it is being processed, and in a way that changes the object. Are you looking at your image on your screen? This is a process that transforms your encoded image into variously coloured dots on your screen, and differs depending on the screen and your settings. Are you copying it to another folder? Another process, which copies bits of your encoded image, checks them, adds data to them and then puts them back, often in the same place, but with bits of information that tell other, future, processes that it is now associated with this other object called a folder. Are you sending a copy to a friend? Yet another process, which copies your encoded image, breaks it up, adds important information to the bits for transferring it over the Internet, and sends the different bits separately, over different channels, via different routes, checking and copying all the way, and reassembling the encoded image at the other end, only to be processed, differently, there, with different fonts, layout and even colours.

Here, in these scenarios, we are only dealing with a stable object – an image to which you have done nothing new. What if you wish to edit the image, change its brightness, its hue, crop it a bit? What you are getting is a whole new object, with each and every change; not only, as with an analogue image, a new object at the end of the process, but a new object with each trivial change. Not only is your encoded image changing, but the bits of it that form its persistent digital object are also changing all the time. Your edits are fundamentally changing the encoding of your image. Its compression is changing; where and how it is stored in memory; it is growing and shrinking, hence the blocks are being reorganized. It is being rendered to your screen using different bits of the processors, of the computer bus, of the drivers. It is constantly using different bits of the application code that renders it to your screen, to your memory, to the processors, *differently*. Though systematic and programmed in every way, always algorithmic, the fashioning of your image is an ongoing, dynamic, transformative metamorphosis.

What this means is that, unlike all the analogue media, in the digital the original impression, the original construction and purpose of the object, doesn't really exist, nor does it really matter. As every rendering, fashioning, of a digital object involves multiple processes fashioning what we see and interact with, we can, if we wish, fashion this encoding any way that our digital devices allow. Not only can we change our images, or any of our digital objects, so that they look different, we can change them fundamentally and fashion them in completely novel ways. We can, if we wished, and if we created the programs that would fashion our digital data this way, *see* our audio files, *hear* our images, graph and diagram our films. We can fashion our own digital data, our online identities, as music, as images, as animations, as statistical reductions, as pure signal, as whatever we like – and whatever our devices can accommodate. With the digital, even if our devices can't accommodate our something new, we can just build new, novel devices that can as they too just process the code. Does this mean that we can do anything? No. But what we can do with digital media is legion compared with other media.

That which is performed on our screens, or on our multitude of devices, even printed from our printers, played from our digital speakers, is not the result of modulating an imprint from an 'original', but of programmatically processing encoded data. We may decide that this processing operates as a modulation from an original, but this is a choice. It is not necessary with the digital. What happens when we simply look at a digital object on one of our many devices – a document, an image, a video, a game or whatever – is that many, many layers of code – programs of instructions – transform our digital object into the thing we see, hear or work with. The digital object is not rendered and modulated into being; it is fashioned into being, fashioned via an enormous number of different actors, transforming the object according to predefined sets of scripts – scripts that can be altered, or even radically different. The performance of a digital object, the viewing of, or interaction with, it on our digital devices, has more in common with the theatre than it does with the cinema, phonograph or television.

Like the theatre, our digital devices draw on a huge number of processes and actors, at all levels, to literally fashion the object anew. For each and every process, no matter how extensive, how central or how trivial, layers upon layers of code – layers upon layers of instructions – are called on to create a new performance each and every time. As with the theatre, these are not fixed renderings of the imprint, but are creative processes where both the process of performance, and the object performed, is different every time. The instructions also can be changed: they are changed with each and every update of an application, each and every time we open our digital object in a different app, on a different device, or send it through a different filter. We can ignore convention and download and use, or even write, new programs that process our code in completely novel and unusual ways. There is no limit, apart from the limits of electronics and algorithms. The objects themselves are constantly re-performed, fundamentally differently from device to device, from system to system. They are never the same. There is no essential relationship between the code and its referent. The digital represents nothing, or, rather, it represents whatever we choose it to represent.

The qualities of the digital

Two stubbornly persistent assumptions about digitality continue to be proffered. First, that the digital is systematic computation. This claim forces digitality as a medium into the background, as though it were not the digital qualities of the object that mattered, but the engineering of the technology. This persistent assumption also focuses the attention on our digital technologies as technologies of the repository, as though only collection, retrieval and computational rendering were what mattered – as though our digital world were merely a vast archive, computationally rendered. However, as I have tried to show in this book, the qualities of the digital are the qualities of media, albeit on steroids. Unlike other media that evoke the archive – selection, preservation, archiving, authority and retrieval – digital media evoke the an-archive: assemblage, translation, fashioning, inclusion and composition.[6]

Throughout this book I have argued that what distinguishes digitality, and its consequences, is not so much the technology, nor its spurious relationship with computation, but the qualities that have been explicit in digitality from its inception – its mediality and performativity. The usual understanding of the digital is as the consequence of a computational biography that led to vast information repositories of 'things' that gain their importance from our ability to reference them – that the significance of the digital is its power to emulate and compute the archive. What we overlook when we think of the digital as a mere organized computational repository of things that are referred to is that the real power of the digital resides in its digitality – as a medium, a unique medium. For digitality, the media qualities of multiplicity (replication), persistence and mobility are augmented, significantly, by necessary perpetual processing – by performativity.

Though digital media share the qualities of all media – multiplicity, persistence and mobility – the most significant quality of the digital, that which distinguishes it from other media and which has been fundamental since the digital went electronic in the 1960s, is the digital as algorithmic performance – an algorithmic performance that we can control. When we engage with the digital, be it a mere image, video or document, or using our Reddit or Pinterest page, even talking on our phone or listening to music, we are not engaging with the outcome of a process, we are engaging with a process itself. Many things that we engage with are the outcomes of processes: chairs, books, cars, newspapers, TV programmes, even our digital devices, are all the outcome of diverse design, production and marketing processes. However, when we engage with a digital object we certainly engage with outcomes of these types of processes as well, through the technical devices, software and Internet systems, but we mostly engage with digital processes. With the digital object there is never an outcome, just a process. Every time you open an object on your digital device, however simple, you are not accessing a stable object, but initiating an ongoing algorithmic performance that, because of the nature of digital performance, is never exactly the same, and is often very different.

Contrary to the usual concept of what the digital is – ephemeral yet stable – the digital object is very, even extraordinarily, persistent by virtue of its multiplicity, and is at the same time capricious in that it is never rendered the same way. Even on the same device, if you open an image it will process the digital code, using other digital code, taking into account the screen settings, brightness and application settings that may have changed. Even if the settings have not changed, the continuous process of rendering the image on your screen will use different memory locations, different processing gates and even, these days, draw on different environmental information, as well as reacting to your use of it at that moment. The opening of an object may open channels of communication with others, including watchful corporations and governmental departments. Nor is variable rendering and process limited, in the digital, to these external or instrumental inputs and surveillances, but each digital object is by default mutable, transformable. Almost every digital application, since those first applications on Engelbart's NLS, has taken for granted that the objects it creates are editable, croppable, pasteable, combinable, shareable, mashable. Today's operating systems (OS), recognizing the essentialness of this quality, include these as core features in the operating system itself. This quality of the digital is its essential and necessary quality of process and transfiguration. What makes the digital digital is merely two-state, synchronous encoding – that's it, and this is neither new nor, in and of itself, significant. However, insofar as the decisions of history were to 'go digital', inevitable commitments ensued.

It would be a mistake to think that the developments in the digital recounted here somehow made the devices in our pockets, in our bags and on our desks, or how we use them, inevitable. Baudot's code did not cause the telecommunications revolution of the late nineteenth and early twentieth centuries, nor did IBM's punched cards cause the data storage revolution at the end of the Second World War. The work of Engelbart and Kay did not cause the interfaces of our phones, pads, laptops or the increasingly rare PCs. These culminations of history were not inevitable and could have been otherwise.

That the importance of the digital is in its digitality, rather than within computation, and that digitality is primarily defined by these qualities, significantly changes our understanding of what the vast Internet archive is and what it is for. The view of the digital as a mere repository of 'things' that we simply 'refer to' focuses the debates of digital collections on issues of selection, preservation, archiving, authority, retrieval and ownership. However, as I have tried to show, the real power and significance of the digital is in its potential as a multiplicitous, pliant and manifold medium. Like previous media, digital media are media of communication. Unlike previous media, digital media are media that in their essence insist on distribution of copies that are never stable, as they are always in the process of being fashioned, and never fixed, as they are always and necessarily *in process*.

Earlier I spoke of the evening of 21 October 1878 when, at the Paris Exposition Universelle, the Grande Médaille d'Or was awarded to two technologies that would become central to our digital world today. Alexander Graham Bell, Elisha Gray and Thomas Edison were each awarded a Grande Médaille d'Or for their independent work on the telephone. At the same ceremony, Jean-Maurice-Émile Baudot was awarded a Grande Médaille d'Or for his development of the Baudot telegraph and its digital encoding. Over the course of the intervening years, the encounters between these technologies, with many others, would culminate in the mobile, netted, digital media world we live in today. What started as a couple of telecommunication technologies which shared the same infrastructure, designed for sharing information, news and conversations between individual people, was, a hundred years later, cobbled together with a group of technologies which processed and extended the message encoding of the telegraph, in almost unlimited ways, through hi-tech relays. This jumble was extended by connecting up the digital devices via the existing telephone and telegraph network. Later were added some junk bands of radio signals, another technology for message transmission and reception, which allowed not only for mobilization of the telephone, but for mobilization and distribution of media creation and use. This mishmash of technologies is what has become the most powerful media technology of all time.

This is not a utopian view – none of this was, is or will be inevitable. There are other alternatives; it could have been otherwise. However, whatever the consequences of history, the digital has always been about messages, about sharing, conversing, interacting and disseminating, about individuals creating. The digital is and always has been a creative medium, but a personal creative medium; not, as many broad-cast media are, one to many, but more intimately, one to one – or many to many. Neither is the digital computational. True, its roots are in engineering, in augmentation of telecommunications. The roots of computers are in mathematics, but in mathematical logic, not computation. As a medium, it has always been more about the social than the virtual. As I hope these historical asides have shown, computers and the digital are not mathematizations of the human condition, but mediations and augmentations of our social needs and desires, algorithmically performed. Digital, it turns out, is not compu-tation; it is the loose amalgam of technologies and practices that have emerged from an encoding of mere presences and absences – and its consequences.

GLOSSARY

Algorithm

An algorithm is a set of strict, self-contained, step-by-step, conditional instructions that must begin somewhere and must end at some point. Continuous loops are not algorithms. We tend to think of algorithms as hyper-mathematical nemeses that control our lives, or at least our economy. It is true that there are some algorithms that do this, but, in fact, *all* computer programs are algorithms. However, any process that is governed by a strict instruction set, that begins with some basic conditions and ends at some point, is an algorithm. (1) Boil water. (2) If boiled, pour in cup; else wait. (3) Add tea bag. (4) If 5 minutes, take tea bag out; else wait. (5) Drink tea, end, is an algorithm.

The term *algorithm* comes from Muhammad ibn Mūsā al-Khwārizmī, a twelfth-century Persian mathematician, who gave us the first book on algebra. Al-Khwārizmī's name was latinized to Algoritmi, and his algebra, as well as his conditional step-by-step mathematical models, were named after him – algebra and algorithm.

Analogue

Analogue media and devices refer to those recording technologies that recorded a continuous signal as an analogue of the thing being recorded. Some examples might help here. The phonograph, or LP vinyl record, would record sound by etching the sound waves onto grooves in the vinyl disc. The etched patterns on the grooves on the vinyl disc are not sound, but they are an analogue of sound and can be replayed back as sound.

Analogue computers, which still exist, though rare, would calculate by using voltages as analogues of quantities. So if you wanted to add 2 + 5 on an analogue computer, you simply increase the voltage on a circuit to 2 units, then increase the voltage again by 5 units, and read the result, 7 units. Computing and calculating in this way is extremely accurate and very fast, much faster and more accurate than digital computers.

Binary

Binary can refer to any number of systems and objects. There are binary stars, binary relations, binary encoding and binary numbers. Basically, binary refers to any relationship or system that has just two states – where there are only two possible conditions that the members of the system or relationship can have. For example, a binary number can only be expressed as a 0 or a 1, none of the other numerals are possible. A binary star is where two stars are interacting, usually violently, together.

For our purposes here, we use binary to refer only to binary numbers. Though technically we could say that digital encoding is a binary system, ons and offs, and it is, it is too often confused with binary numbers, which it is not.

Bitmapped graphics

Bitmapped graphics is what we see every time we look at our computer screen, our pad or our phone. Even if you have a non-smart phone, your screen is bitmapped, as is just about any display device today. All of our screens are made up of a bunch of dots in a very fine grid. As our computer turns on a dot, giving it a colour, so it shines with that colour. The mapping comes from the pattern of dots that make up what we want to see – a letter, an icon, an image, part of a window, whatever.

All digital images, whatever they are, are also bitmaps. Your images are simply grids of dots, lots and lots of them, as are your videos. Digital samples the world in bits, dots, and stores these dots as codes. When your computer wants to draw a window or anything on your screen, it creates a bitmap of that via a program and renders it as dots on your screen.

Character codes

Character codes are the earliest form of digital encoding. Starting with a 5-bit code, the capital letters of the Latin alphabet, many other alphabets were added. It wasn't until the mid-twentieth century that character encodings included lower-case letters, and it wasn't until the 1980s, with Unicode, that there was a character encoding that could accommodate all printable characters, old and new (see Chapter Two).

Computation

Computation has been extended to mean many things today. In contemporary computer science, it refers to any process that can be expressed as an algorithm – any computer program, for example. However, its primary meaning is to *compute, calculate* or *render*. It is a mathematical, or rather arithmetic, concept that refers to calculating with numbers. The actual calculation, as has been the case for over 200 years, would always follow a set of formal instructions (see Algorithm), but computation itself refers to the calculations.

Computer
The devices that we use today, that we still call computers, were associated with the name first by Alan Turing (see Chapter Three). With his hypothetical Universal Turing Device, he showed that he could create a mechanical device that, in principle, could do any calculation that people could do (see Computor). The name stuck, not least as the early computers were designed to do the work that people had been doing up to that point. Today we still call these devices computers, even though little of what they do relates to calculation or what the human computors were doing.

Computor
Computors, sometimes referred to as *computers*, were people. From the late eighteenth century, the need to calculate and compute numbers for all sorts of problems (astronomical, cartological, sociological, financial, military and so on) was growing rapidly and was filled by a large group of professional calculators. These calculators were people who calculated, as a coordinated group, usually for governments. This was the origin of computation as both a process and a concept.

CRT
A CRT, or cathode ray tube, is the display tube that all of our TVs and display monitors had before flat screens. However, they were analogue devices, unlike our flat-screen LCDs or LEDs which are digital, even when they were connected to our computers. Though they too displayed images as a grid of dots (see Bitmapped graphics), the way they modulated the dots was completely different than how we generate our images on screens today. They were, however, an important technology for the callow age of computers and computer interaction.

Digital
Well, this is what this book is about. Digital, the term, can mean many things. Digital does refer to one of the numerals from 0 to 9. It also can be used to refer to our fingers (including our thumbs), and even the keys of any keyboard musical instrument. However, here, we are interested in digital as it has come to refer to an encoding of just two states – on or off. As seems almost universally the case, digital is often wrongly represented as 1s and 0s. Though 1s and 0s are encoded digitally, as

are all the other numbers, digital does not encode things by 1s or 0s, but literally by presences and absences, which can be interpreted by a computer chip as *ons* or *offs*.

Digital encoding is the simplest of all possible encodings, hence its potential. It is impossible to encode anything with just one state, *on* for instance, hence everything would be the same and offer no means of encoding difference. Two states offers the maximum possibility for simplicity and lack of redundancy, while allowing for any form of inscription, media expression, to be encoded.

However, to be created, displayed, used or manipulated, digital code must be processed. This is done via integrated circuits of transistors, microprocessors (chips) using algorithms – many, many, many layers of algorithms, or what we call operating systems, programs and apps.

Digitality — Something that is in the state or condition of being digital.

Encoding — Encoding simply means to translate something into a code. Here, we have been concerned with digital codes, where, initially, only letters were encoded. However, as we all know, from the 1950s and '60s, all sorts of media have been encoded with digital codes – images, video, models, complex documents, data, signals and so on.

Logic gate — A logic gate is a switch that makes a decision. All of our digital computers not only use logic gates, but all of their processing is dependent on large arrays of these logic gates. Today, logic gates are tiny transistors assembled on chips, but they all work basically the same. There are a number of logic gates that make different 'decisions'. Some might be AND gates, or OR gates, or NOT gates, but there are also other types such as NAND, NOR, XOR and XNOR. The combination of these gates, literally switches that open or close a circuit depending on the input and the kind of logic gate, is what makes our computer work.

Media — Media usually refers to the large number of technologies and enterprises that make up mass media: television, radio, newspapers, mail, websites, even billboards. However, media is more extensive than this, and also refers to the actual material and systems we use to record our expressions, memories and information. Not only is the television or radio signal a medium, but so is paper and ink, paint, photographic prints and negatives,

	phonographic disks, magnetic disks and tape, etched dots on plastic DVDs and so on. Anything that can carry, in perpetuity, our expressions, and be 'read' again, operates as a medium.
Memory (Computer)	We are probably all aware when we buy a new laptop, pad or phone that we need a reasonable amount of memory to store our data, our music, messages and apps. We are often aware that there are two types of memory on our devices, storage and memory. Actually, both are memory, or both are storage, depending on how you look at it. Storage tends to refer to stable memory, the place where we put our apps, data, music, videos, documents, whatever, the things that we want to keep even if our device is off or out of power. These days, our storage may also include a number of external stores, including cloud storage. Memory tends to refer to what used to be called RAM (random-access memory). This is the working memory of the device, where it is putting all the code and data that it is working on at that moment. These two are what make up our memory on our digital devices.
Microprocessor	A microprocessor is a complex array of transistors (switches or logic gates) that is the core of our digital devices. Microprocessors are the tiny square bit hidden in our device (actually our devices will have a number of microprocessors), that actually does the work of processing the code that does everything on our digital devices.
	Originally, computers were very large arrays of vacuum tubes which did the work of the switches (logic gates). This is what often led to computers the size of houses. By 1971, engineers at several companies had managed to miniaturize these logic gates to tiny transistors (see Transistor), which could put those houses of vacuum tubes on a square the size of your thumbnail. It was this development that led almost instantly to the rise of the personal computer.
Relay	A relay is the simplest form of a logic gate, or switch. A relay is simply a metal switch that is controlled by an electromagnet. Turn on the electromagnet with a circuit and it would pull a metal plate either opening or closing another circuit, just like a light switch. Relays are a very old form of electronic switch, and were used in the first electronic calculators and computers, as well as the very first telegraphs. Though perfectly good for the telegraphs, and a host of other electronic devices,

they proved far too slow as computer switches, and were replaced by vacuum tubes which did the same job, but faster (see also Transistor).

Telegraph   The telegraph, first perfected in the 1830s and '40s, was a means of sending text messages over a wire with a code. The first successful telegraph used Morse's equipment and code. However, many telegraphs were developed and used throughout the nineteenth and twentieth centuries. From the beginning of the twentieth century, roughly from 1920, all telegraphs have been encoded using a digital code, that of Baudot and Murray. Telegraphs were once as common as SMS is today.

Teletype   Teletype, or telex, was a telegraph system developed in the 1920s, but became a common form of interoffice communications, much as our email is today, from the late 1940s. Teletype or telex is a telegraph, using digital codes, which connects two or more teletypewriters/printers. When a message was typed into one tele-typewriter, and then sent, it was sent as a digital code directly over existing telephone wires to the receiving teleprinters, which would print out the message on a roll of paper.

Transistor   Transistors are merely a solid-state switch, basically a switch like a relay, but with no moving parts (see also Relay and Logic gate). The first transistors were developed at the beginning of the twentieth century, but the viable versions did not appear until the 1940s and 1950s. Transistors can be made to be extremely small and extremely fast. They are also very durable and do not burn out like other switches. For computers transistors were incorporated into the early electronic computers like MIT's TX2, but they were not incorporated into integrated circuits, microprocessors, until the early 1970s. The continued miniaturization of transistors, and the integrated circuits that they make up, has led to the increasing power and speed of our digital devices over the past 45 years.

Vacuum tube   Vacuum tubes are also known as electron tubes, just tubes in North America, or valves in Britain. A vacuum tube is a glass tube with a base, much like an electric light bulb from which it developed, that controls an electric current between electrodes in a vacuum. In the vacuum tube, electricity can only pass from one electrode to another, in one direction. By adding metal grids between the electrodes, and adding a current to these grids, the vacuum tube can act as a very fast switch

– add electric current to the grid and turn the flow
of electricity between the electrodes on or off.

The problem with vacuum tubes was, and is, that
they get very hot and burn out quickly. This makes them
a very unreliable switch and is why they were replaced
by very fast, and very reliable, transistors as soon as they
were available (see Transistor).

WIMPS   All of our digital displays use WIMPs today, and have
done since the mid-1980s. WIMP refers to Windows,
Icons, Menus, Pointers. Though today we don't even
notice these features on our screens, in the early 1980s,
they were novel and not completely self-evident. However,
with Apple's Lisa (1979) and then Macintosh (1984) and
Microsoft's Windows (1985) working on computers in
windows, with icons and menus for functions, and
pointers (mice, touchpads, touch screens), this way of
displaying what we are doing on computers has become
ubiquitous.

WYSIWYG   It is hard to believe that there was a time when, if you
wrote something on a computer, it was a difficult
process. When I was writing my MA thesis, in 1982,
I wrote it on a mainframe text editor. I had to write it
one line at a time, and use complex codes to edit the
lines. I could not see all the text at once, and it didn't
look anything like what I would print out. If I wanted
to print it out with good fonts, bold, italics and different
text sizes, I would have to program the text directly to
tell a printer what to do. WYSIWYG changed all that.

WYSIWYG refers to 'what you see is what you get'.
Today, WYSIWYG is pervasive. We would be horrified if
we typed some text, or worked on an image, and it didn't
look like what we would transmit or print. Yet with the
first WYSIWYG editors from the mid-1970s there was
resistance to this form of working as a 'dumbing down'
of proper text formatting.

REFERENCES

INTRODUCTION

1 Nicholas Negroponte, *Being Digital* (New York, 1995), p. 4.
2 Gilbert Ryle, *The Concept of Mind* (London, 1949).

1 DIGITAL CODES, TICKER TAPE, PUNCHED CARDS AND TELEPRINTING:
ON THE ORIGIN OF DIGITALITY

1 Wikipedia search results for 'Digital', en.wikipedia.org/wiki/Digital, accessed 5 September 2014.
2 Samuel Morse, *Samuel F. B. Morse, His Letters and Journals: Edited and Supplemented by his Son Edward Lind Morse*, 2 vols (New York, 1914).
3 Ibid.
4 Engineer-in-Chief's Office, *Technical Pamphlets for Workmen, Subject: Hughes Type-Printing Telegraph* (London, 1919).
5 The Administration des Télégraphes was merged with the French Post Office in 1879 to become Postes, Télégraphes et Téléphones – the famous PTT. Since 1991, the French PTT has been known by its current name, Le Poste.
6 Though I have shown, and will show again, that digital is not binary numbers, I will use the conventional mode of writing digital as 1s and 0s.
7 Remington would go on to become Remington Rand, one of the leading IT companies of the 1950s, '60s and '70s.
8 G. E. Wood, *Telegraphs: High Speed Committee Report, 1913–1914*, POST 30/3589B (British Telecommunications Archives, 1916); 'Report of Committee Appointed to Consider the Question of High-Speed Telegraphy', *Post Office Electrical Engineers' Journal*, X (1914), pp. 1–2.
9 Quoted in Ken Beauchamp, *History of Telegraphy* (London, 2001), p. 391.
10 Samuel Morse writing to his partner, F. Smith, in 1838. Quoted in Laura Otis, *Networking: Communicating with Bodies and Machines in the Nineteenth Century* (Ann Arbor, MI, 2011), p. 120.

2 DATA ENCODING AND STORAGE BEFORE THE COMPUTER

1   'Broken telephone' refers to the gossip game that is also known as 'Chinese whispers' in the UK.
2   Eric Fischer, 'The Evolution of Character Codes, 1874–1968', citeseerx.ist. psu.edu, 1 September 2014.
3   Ada Lovelace, *Sketch of the Analytical Engine* (London, 1842).
4   Before the Second World War, it seems that Watson approved, and may have even negotiated, an extremely successful contract between IBM's German subsidiary and the Nazi regime. Even during the war, IBM maintained supplies of punched cards to Dehomag, its German subsidiary, through its suppliers in occupied Europe. The allegations are covered in Edwin Black, *IBM and the Holocaust* (Washington, DC, 2001).
5   Joseph D. Becker, *Unicode 88* (Palo Alto, CA, 1988).

3 REVISITING COMPUTATION: COMPUTATION DOESN'T NEED TO BE DIGITAL

1   T.T.P.B. Warren, 'On the Applications of the Calculating Machine of M. Thomas de Colmar to Electrical Computations', *Journal of the Society of Telegraph Engineers*, I (1872), pp. 141–67 (p. 164).
2   Ibid., p. 165.
3   A major concern of social demographics and social statistics from the end of the nineteenth century was, unfortunately, with racial 'characteristics' and 'potentials'. Race was implicated in all characterizations then of human populations at this time, with, as we now know, disastrous consequences.
4   Ibid., p. 167.
5   H. A. Travers, 'The Network Calculator Brought Up to Date', *Westinghouse Engineer*, IV (1944), pp. 111–14.
6   H. L. Hazen, O. R. Schurig and M. F. Gardner, 'The M.I.T. Network Analyzer Design and Application to Power System Problems', *Transactions of the AIEEE* (July 1930), pp. 1102–13.
7   Aristotle Tympas, 'From Digital to Analog and Back: The Ideology of Intelligent Machines in the History of the Electrical Analyzer, 1870s–1960s', IEEE *Annals of the History of Computing*, XVIII (1996), pp. 42–8 (p. 45).
8   Vannevar Bush, *Pieces of the Action* (New York, 1970), p. 161.
9   In one article (Vannevar Bush, F. D. Gage and H. R. Stewart, 'A Continuous Integraph', *Journal of the Franklin Institute*, CCIII (1927), pp. 63–84), Bush described the device as a 'continuous *integraph*'. In a second article, four years later, we find him using the term 'Differential Analyzer' (Vannevar Bush, 'The Differential Analyzer: A New Machine for Solving Differential Equations', *Journal of the Franklin Institute*, CCXII (1931), pp. 447–88).
10 Vannevar Bush, 'As We May Think', *Atlantic Monthly*, CLXXVI (1945), pp. 101–8.
11 Michael K. Buckland, 'Emanuel Goldberg, Electronic Document Retrieval, and Vannevar Bush's Memex', *Journal of the American Society for Information Science*,

XLIII (1992), pp. 284–94; Matt Kaz, 'Vannevar Bush and Memex, The World Wide Web: The Beginning and Now', www-personal.umich.edu, accessed 11 May 2015; Stephen Davies, 'Still Building the Memex', *Communications of the* ACM, LIV (2011), pp. 80–88; Wikipedia, Memex, en.wikipedia.org.

12 Bush, 'As We May Think', p. 106.

13 Only with the invention of the microchip, which powers all of our computers today, were engineers able to pack a very large number of transistors into an incredibly small space giving a large number of logic gates that were close together, allowing for the massive processing speeds we get today.

14 Richard Elen, 'TV Technology 10: Roll VTR', www.screenonline.org.uk, accessed 22 June 2015.

15 Alan Turing, 'On Computable Numbers, with an Application to the Entschei-dungsproblem', *Proceedings of the London Mathematical Society*, ser. 2, XLII (1937), pp. 230–65.

16 Ibid., p. 231.

17 M. Mitchell Waldrop, 'Claude Shannon: Reluctant Father of the Digital Age', www.technologyreview.com, accessed 19 May 2015.

18 Eugene Chiu, Jocelyn Lin, Brok Mcferron, Noshirwan Petigara and Satwiksai Seshasai, 'A Mathematical Theory of Claude Shannon: A Study of the Style and Context of his Work up to the Genesis of Information Theory', *Communication: Bell System Technical Journal*, XXVII (2001), pp. 379–423, p. 26.

19 Claude Shannon, 'Communication Theory of Secrecy Systems', *Bell System Technical Journal*, XXVIII (1949), p. 689.

20 This article was first written as a classified report, 'A Mathematical Theory of Cryptography, Memorandum MM 45-110-02', of 1 September 1945 for Bell Laboratories. After the war, the report was declassified and published in 1949 as Shannon, 'Communication Theory of Secrecy Systems'.

21 Excerpt of a letter from Shannon to Bush, 16 February 1939. Library of Congress.

22 Harry Nyquist, 'Certain Factors Affecting Telegraph Speed', *Bell Labs Technical Journal*, III (1924), pp. 324–46.

23 Ralph Hartley, 'Transmission of Information', *Bell Labs Technical Journal*, VII (1928), pp. 535–63.

24 Ibid., p. 536.

25 Claude Shannon, 'A Mathematical Theory of Communication', *Bell System Technical Journal*, XXVII (1948), pp. 379–423, 623–56.

4 BACK TO CONTENT: FROM COMPUTATION TO MEDIA

1 For a discussion of who Vladimir Zworykin was and his achievements see his Wikipedia entry, en.wikipedia.org. For a very simple discussion of how his iconoscope and kinescope worked see www.videoeditingsage.com/vladi-mir-zworykin.html.

2 For a simple early history of television, from the BBC's point of view, see their site, www.bbc.co.uk/historyofthebbc. For a very interesting historical take

on the early history of television see RCA's 1956 documentary, 'The Story of Television', www.youtube.com/watch?v=NxbdMlıflUc.

3 Norman Taylor, in 'Retrospectives: The Early Years in Computer Graphics at MIT, Lincoln Lab and Harvard', ed. Jan Hurst, SIGGRAPH '89 Panel Proceedings (1989), pp. 20–25, here at p. 20.

4 John von Neumann, 'Memorandum on the Program of the High-Speed Computer Project, November 8, 1945', quoted in Herman Goldstine, The Computer: From Pascal to von Neumann (Princeton, NJ, 1972), p. 242.

5 Taylor, 'Retrospectives', p. 20.

6 Charles W. Adams, 'Small Problems on Large Computers', ACM '52: Proceedings of the 1952 ACM National Meeting (Pittsburgh) (1952), pp. 99–102 (p. 101).

7 John T. Gilmore, 'Retrospectives II: The Early Years in Computer Graphics', ACM SIGGRAPH Computer Graphics, 23 (1989), pp. 39–73.

8 Ivan E. Sutherland, 'Sketchpad, a Man–Machine Graphical Communication System', PhD thesis, MIT, 1963.

9 Doug Engelbart, 'Augmenting Human Intellect: A Conceptual Framework. Summary Report AFOSR-3233', Stanford Research Institute (Stanford, CA, 1962), p. 1.

10 Ibid., p. 8.

11 Ibid., p. 89.

12 The opening lines from the transcript of Doug Engelbart's 1968 demo.

13 Ibid.

14 Steven Levy, Insanely Great: The Life and Times of Macintosh, the Computer that Changed Everything (New York, 1994).

15 Ted Nelson, 'File Structure for the Complex, the Changing, and the Indeterminate', Association for Computing Machinery: Proceedings of the 20th National Conference (1965), pp. 84–100.

16 Ted Nelson, Computer Lib / Dream Machines (Chicago, IL, 1974), Dream Machines, p. 45.

17 Howard Rheingold, 'Tools for Thought', www.rheingold.com, accessed 12 September 2015.

18 R. Lucky, Lucky Strikes . . . Again (Feats and Foibles of Engineers) (New York, 1993). Quoted in Information Theory and the Digital Age, ed. O. Aftab, P. Cheung, A. Kim, S. Thakkar and N. Yeddanapudi (Cambridge, MA, 2001), p. 19.

19 Aftab et al., eds, Information Theory and the Digital Age, pp. 9–11.

20 Alan Kay, 'Personal Computing', paper presented at the meeting '20 Years of Computer-Science', Istituto di Elaborazione dell'Informazione, Pisa, Italy (1975).

21 Alan Kay, 'The Early History of Smalltalk', Association for Computing Machinery: Proceedings of the Second ACM SIGPLAN Conference on History of Programming Languages (1993), pp. 69–95, p. 76.

22 Ibid.

23 Ibid.

24 Alan Kay and Adele Goldberg, 'Personal Dynamic Media', Computer, X (1977), pp. 31–41.

25 Ibid., pp. 31–2.

26 For a more comprehensive, and more accurate, history of the early
    interactions between Apple and Xerox PARC, see Malcolm Gladwell's
    well-documented critique of this history: Malcolm Gladwell, 'Creation Myth:
    Xerox PARC, Apple, and the Truth about Innovation', New Yorker, 16 May 2011.
    For a more considered take on why Xerox didn't capitalize on the work of
    their own PARC researchers, see Arun Rao and Piero Scaruffi, 'Lab Inventors:
    Xerox PARC and the Innovation Machine (1969–83)', in A History of Silicon
    Valley: The Largest Creation of Wealth in the History of the Planet: A Moral Tale, ed.
    Arun Rao and Piero Scaruffi (Palo Alto, CA, 2011).
27 Kay, 'Personal Computing', p. 23.

5 MEDIA CLONES, MULTIPLE RENDERINGS: THE CONSEQUENCES OF THE DIGITAL

1 John B. Kennedy, 'When Woman is Boss: An Interview with Nikola Tesla',
   Collier's Magazine, January 30, 1926, www.tfcbooks.com, accessed 6 October
   2015.
2 Lewis Dartnell, 'The Digital Black Hole: Will it Delete Your Memories?',
   The Guardian, 16 February 2015.
3 Jacques Derrida, 'Signature Event Context', in Margins of Philosophy, trans.
   Alan Bass (Chicago, IL, 1985), p. 314.
4 Bruno Latour, Science in Action: How to Follow Scientists and Engineers through
   Society (Cambridge, MA, 1987).
5 Hi-fi is the high-fidelity equipment used to play vinyl phonograph records.
   The quality of the sound of a vinyl record is dependent on the electronics
   of these hi-fis.
6 For a full treatment of the an-archive see Eivind Røssaak, ed., The Archive in
   Motion: New Conceptions of the Archive in Contemporary Thought and New Media
   Practices (Oslo, 2010).

SELECT BIBLIOGRAPHY

Abbate, Janet, *Inventing the Internet* (Cambridge, MA, 1999)
—, *Recoding Gender: Women's Changing Participation in Computing* (Cambridge, MA, 2012)
ACM SIGGRAPH 89 *Panel Proceedings* (New York, 1989)
Aftab, O., P. Cheung, A. Kim, S. Thakkar and N. Yeddanapudi, eds, *Information Theory and the Digital Age* (Cambridge, MA, 2001)
Agar, Jon, 'Introduction: History of Computing: Approaches, New Directions and the Possibility of Informatic History', *History and Technology: An International Journal*, XV (1998), pp. 1–5
Akera, Atsushi, *Calculating a Natural World: Scientists, Engineers, and Computers during the Rise of U.S. Cold War Research* (Cambridge, MA, 2008)
Aspray, William, ed., *Computing before Computers* (Ames, IA, 1990)
Barnes, Susan, 'Alan Kay, Transforming the Computer into a Communication Medium', *IEEE Annals of the History of Computing*, XXIX/2 (2007), pp. 18–30
Beauchamp, Ken, *A History of Telegraphy: Its Technology and Application* (London, 2001)
Becker, Joseph D., *Unicode 88* (Palo Alto, CA, 1988)
Buckland, Michael K., 'Emanuel Goldberg, Electronic Document Retrieval, and Vannevar Bush's Memex', *Journal of the American Society for Information Science*, XLIII (1992), pp. 284–94
Bush, Vannevar, 'The Differential Analyzer. A New Machine for Solving Differential Equations', *Journal of the Franklin Institute*, CCXII (1931)
—, 'Memex Revisited', in *Science is Not Enough*, ed. Vannevar Bush (New York, 1967)
—, 'As We May Think', *The Atlantic Monthly*, CLXXVI (1945), pp. 101–8
Bush, Vannevar, F. D. Gage and H. R. Stewart, 'A Continuous Integraph', *Journal of the Franklin Institute*, CCIII (1927)
Calvert, J. B., 'The Electromagnetic Telegraph', http://mysite.du.edu/, 2000
Campbell-Kelly, Martin, and William Aspray, *Computer: A History of the Information Machine* (Boulder, CO, 1996)
Ceruzzi, Paul E., *A History of Modern Computing* (Cambridge, MA, 1998)
Chiu, Eugene, Jocelyn Lin, Brok Mcferron, Noshirwan Petigara and Satwiksai Seshasai, 'A Mathematical Theory of Claude Shannon: A Study of the Style and Context of his Work up to the Genesis of Information Theory', *Communication: Bell System Technical Journal*, XXVII (2001), pp. 379–423

Chun, Wendy Hui Kyong, *Programmed Visions: Software and Memory* (Cambridge, MA, 2011)

Cortada, James W., *The Digital Hand, Volume 1: How Computers Changed the Work of American Manufacturing, Transportation, and Retail Industries* (Oxford, 2004)

—, *The Digital Hand, Volume 2: How Computers Changed the Work of American Financial, Telecommunications, Media, and Entertainment Industries* (Oxford, 2006)

—, *The Digital Hand, Volume 3: How Computers Changed the Work of American Public Sector Industries* (Oxford, 2008)

Davies, Stephen, 'Still Building the Memex', *Communications of the* ACM, LIV (2011), pp. 80–88

Edwards, Paul N., *The Closed World: Computers and the Politics of Discourse in Cold War America* (Cambridge, MA, 1997)

Elen, Richard, 'TV Technology 10. Roll VTR', www.screenonline.org.uk, 22 June 2015

Engelbart, Doug, 'Augmenting Human Intellect: A Conceptual Framework. Summary Report AFOSR-3233', Stanford Research Institute (Stanford, CA, 1962)

Engineer-in-Chief's Office, *Technical Pamphlets for Workmen, Subject: Hughes Type-Printing Telegraph* (London, 1919)

Ensmenger, Nathan L., *The Computer Boys Take Over: Computers, Programmers, and the Politics of Technical Expertise* (Cambridge, MA, 2010)

Fischer, Eric, 'The Evolution of Character Codes, 1874–1968', citeseerx.ist.psu. edu, 1 September 2014

Ford, Paul, 'What Is Code?', www.bloomberg.com, 11 June 2015

Frouin, André, 'Obituary: Emile Baudot', *Journal Télégraphique*, XXVII (1903)

Gilmore, John T., 'Retrospectives 11: The Early Years in Computer Graphics', ACM SIGGRAPH *Computer Graphics*, XXIII (1989), pp. 39–73

Gladwell, Malcolm 'Creation Myth: Xerox PARC, Apple, and the Truth about Innovation', *The New Yorker*, 16 May 2011

Grier, David Alan, *When Computers Were Human* (Princeton, NJ, 2005)

Haigh, Thomas, 'Actually, Turing Did Not Invent the Computer', *Communications of the* ACM, LVII (2014), pp. 36–41

—, 'Inventing Information Systems: The Systems Men and the Computer, 1950–1968', *Business History Review*, LXXV (2001), pp. 15–61

Hartley, Ralph, 'Transmission of Information', *Bell Labs Technical Journal*, VII (1928), pp. 535–63

Hazen, H. L., O. R. Schurig and M. F. Gardner, 'The M.I.T. Network Analyzer Design and Application to Power System Problems', *Transactions of the* AIEEE (July 1930), pp. 1102–113

Kay, Alan, 'Personal Computing', paper presented at the Meeting '20 Years of Computer-Science', Istituto di Elaborazione dell'Informazione, Pisa, Italy (1975), pp. 2–30

—, 'The Early History of Smalltalk', *Association for Computing Machinery: Proceedings of the Second* ACM SIGPLAN *Conference on History of Programming Languages* (1993), pp. 69–95

Kay, Alan, and Adele Goldberg, 'Personal Dynamic Media', *Computer*, x (1977), pp. 31–41

Kaz, Matt, 'Vannevar Bush and Memex, The World Wide Web: The Beginning and Now', www-personal.umich.edu, 11 May 2015

Kennedy, John B., 'When Woman is Boss: An Interview with Nikola Tesla', *Collier's Magazine*, 30 January 1926

Levy, Steven, *Insanely Great: The Life and Times of Macintosh, the Computer That Changed Everything* (New York, 1994)

Lovelace, Ada, *Sketch of the Analytical Engine* (London, 1842)

Lundberg, Kent, 'The History of Analog Computing – Introduction to the Special Section', *IEEE Control Systems Magazine* (June 2005), pp. 22–8

Mahoney, Michael S. 'The History of Computing in the History of Technology', *Annals of the History of Computing*, x (1988) pp. 113–25

Morse, Samuel F. B., *His Letters and Journals: Edited and Supplemented by his Son Edward Lind Morse*, 2 vols (New York, 1914)

Negroponte, Nicholas, *Being Digital* (New York, 1995)

Nelson, Ted, 'File Structure for the Complex, the Changing, and the Indeterminate', *Association for Computing Machinery: Proceedings of the 20th National Conference* (1965), pp. 84–100

—, *Computer Lib / Dream Machines* (Chicago, IL, 1974)

Nyquist, Harry, 'Certain Factors Affecting Telegraph Speed', *Bell Labs Technical Journal*, III (1924), pp. 324–46

Otis, Laura, *Networking: Communicating with Bodies and Machines in the Nineteenth Century* (Ann Arbor, MI, 2011)

Pendry, H. W., *The Baudot Printing Telegraph System* (London, 1919)

Randell, Brian, ed., *The Origins of Digital Computers: Selected Papers* (Berlin, 1982), pp. 125–33. See Chapter 3, 'Tabulating Machines', which has excerpts of Hollerith's 1889 *An Electric Tabulating System* and Couffignal's 1933 *Calculating Machines: Their Principles and Evolution*

Rao, Arun, and Piero Scaruffi, 'Lab Inventors: Xerox PARC and the Innovation Machine (1969–83)', in *A History of Silicon Valley: The Largest Creation of Wealth in the History of the Planet: A Moral Tale*, ed. Arun Rao and Piero Scaruffi (Palo Alto, CA, 2011)

Rheingold, Howard, 'Tools for Thought', www.rheingold.com, accessed 12 September 2015

Savage, Neil, 'Information Theory after Shannon', *Communications of the ACM*, LIV (2011), pp. 16–18

Seely Brown, John, and Paul Duguid, 'Local Knowledge: Innovation in the Networked Age', *Management Learning*, XXXIII (2002), pp. 427–38

Shannon, Claude, 'A Mathematical Theory of Communication', *Bell System Technical Journal*, XXVII (1948), pp. 379–423, 623–56

—, 'A Symbolic Analysis of Relay and Switching Circuits', MA thesis, Massachusetts Institute of Technology, 1936

Sutherland, Ivan E., 'Sketchpad, a Man–Machine Graphical Communication System', PhD thesis, Massachusetts Institute of Technology, 1963

Travers, H. A., 'The Network Calculator Brought up to Date,' *Westinghouse Engineer*, IV (1944), pp. 111–14

Turing, Alan, 'On Computable Numbers, with an Application to the *Entscheidungsproblem*', *Proceedings of the London Mathematical Society*, ser. 2, XLII (1937), pp. 230–65

Turner, Fred, *From Counterculture to Cyberculture: Stewart Brand, the Whole Earth Network, and the Rise of Digital Utopianism* (Chicago, IL, 2006)

Tympas, Aristotle, 'From Digital to Analog and Back: The Ideology of Intelligent Machines in the History of the Electrical Analyzer, 1870s–1960s', *IEEE Annals of the History of Computing*, XVIII (1996), pp. 42–8

von Neumann, John, *First Draft Report on the EDVAC* (Pittsburgh, PA, 1945)

Waldrop, M. Mitchell, 'Claude Shannon: Reluctant Father of the Digital Age', www.technologyreview.com, 19 May 2015

Warren, T.T.P.B., 'On the Applications of the Calculating Machine of M. Thomas de Colmar to Electrical Computations', *Journal of the Society of Telegraph Engineers*, I (1872), pp. 141–67

Winston, Brian, *Media Technology and Society: A History: From the Telegraph to the Internet* (London, 1988)

Woolley, David R., 'PLATO: The Emergence of Online Community', http://thinkofit.com/plato/dwplato.htm, 11 March 2012

ACKNOWLEDGEMENTS

This book has been, inevitably, the outcome of many years of reading, practice, conversation, argument and contemplation. It is, therefore, impossible to thank everyone who has, in some way or another, contributed to this work. However, I would like to single out a few people who, through many encouragements, discussions and debates, have helped with the formation of this book.

I must begin by thanking Jussi Parikka not only for inspiring the approach I have taken in this book, but, without his encouragement, I may never have begun this work. It was also Jussi Parikka who recommended me to my publisher, Reaktion Books. For his never-ending patience, friendship, profound advice and constant inspiration, I thank him.

I must also thank the following students, colleagues and friends who have, in different ways, guided or inspired my attention in many relevant directions. I would like to thank Ramesh Srinivasan, Geoffrey Bowker, David Gauthier, Siva Vaidhyanathan, Daryle Rigney, Steve Hemming, Jim Enote, Dominic Walker and especially the late Susan Leigh Star.

Thanks must also go to my wife, Rosita D'Amora, and my son, Filippo, for their endless patience and understanding. I know it hasn't been easy.

Last, but not least, I would like to thank my editor, Ben Hayes, who has been a pillar of support throughout the writing of this book. I am eternally grateful to Ben, and Reaktion Books, for their belief in this work and in me.

Though I have been profoundly influenced and helped by all mentioned above, I must emphasize that the opinions in this work, and its inevitable errors, are exclusively my own.

PHOTO ACKNOWLEDGEMENTS

Most of the images in this book are from the public domain, but particular thanks must be given to those who generously granted permission to reproduce personal images. Alan Kay kindly allowed me to reproduce the cover image of his 1974 publication, *Personal Computing*, and Theodor Holm Nelson generously granted me permission to reproduce an image from his dual book, *Computer Lib / Dream Machines*. I am sincerely grateful to both of these giants of the discipline for their kind support. I would also like to thank Marty Ritchey of SRI International who promptly granted permission to reproduce the image of Doug Engelbart using the NLS system. Thanks also to the Mitre Corporation for their permission to reproduce the images of both the Whirlwind Project and Ivan Sutherland's later work on Sketchpad.

INDEX

Page numbers in *italics* indicate illustrations